Financial Planning For The Not Yet Wealthy

(What The Average Guy Needs To Know About Money But No One Is Telling Him)

By Antonio Filippone, RFC, FMM
Registered Financial Consultant

DISCLAIMER:

PAST PERFORMANCE IS NO GUARANTEE OF FUTURE RESULTS

The case studies do not reflect actual clients. Any reference to securities is based upon historical data that is public sourced. No statement made herein is to suggest stock market performance or future performance, and no case study is used to imply future performance. The case study is intended to illustrate services available through the adviser. They do not necessarily represent the experience of any clients.

Rockford Retirement Planning, Inc. (RRP) does not offer legal or tax advice. Please consult the appropriate professional regarding your individual circumstance.

Investment Advisory Services offered through Retirement Wealth Advisors, (RWA) a Registered Investment Advisor. RRP and RWA are not affiliated. Investing involves risk including the potential loss of principal. No investment strategy can guarantee a profit or protect against loss in periods of declining values. Opinions expressed are subject to change without notice and are not intended as investment advice or to predict future performance. Past performance does not guarantee future results. Consult your financial professional before making any investment decision,

Many times throughout the book I encourage the reader to get expert help. The ideas in this book are designed to get the reader thinking and then seek out the appropriate professional advice. In no way is this book intended as a stand-alone financial tool but instead it is to be used along with proper guidance from licensed professionals.

Publisher: Ideal Life Publishing
P.O. Box 2698
Loves Park, IL 61132

Publish Date: 1/19/2010
Republish Date: 04/22/2019

ISBN: 978-0-692-00737-2

Contents

Foreword

In today's tough economic times; banks failing, consumer debt is increasing, rising unemployment and huge losses in the stock markets; learning how to manage our money, eliminate debts, establish an emergency fund and planning for your future. This type of planning is imperative to you and your family's survival.

We all must learn new ways to achieve our future goals. The way our parents and grandparents managed their money just will not work for our generation. Too many things have changed! Therefore, we must adapt new strategies and have an open mind while moving forward, so we can truly view new ideas as solutions. If we move forward with a close minded approach, nothing will change and "we will get what we always got!"

All too often, financial authors put books together, full of financial strategies that the average family cannot use! These books are geared for the affluent that live in an entirely different world! They don't have to worry about the same things we worry about. We worry about paying our mortgage, our credit card and putting braces on Mary's teeth. The affluent worry about their stock portfolios and whether they should fly to Europe for the summer! These two worlds are completely separate from each other, so it is not surprising that the financial strategies they use will not work for the average blue collar, hardworking family!

But "Financial Planning for the Not Yet Wealthy"
changes everything.

Finally someone has stepped up to put financial planning and debt management strategies into a simplistic common sense approach that will help families to set and achieve their future goals. "Financial Planning for the Not Yet Wealthy" is going to change the way you look at finance.

Acknowledgments

This book could not have been written without the help of the many positive influences others have had on my life. One of those influences is a man named Lew Nason who about 5 years ago encouraged me to read books that helped me see outside of my box and beyond the typical industry training that I had received. His efforts to broaden my horizons have changed my life and the life of my clients in ways that I never dreamed possible. I want to thank Lew, not only for helping me grow my business but for helping me grow my business in a way that truly helps others so everyone wins. Thank you, Lew, for encouraging me to not just play the part of a professional as so many in our industry do, but to actually seek out the knowledge and to become one.

I also want to say a word of thanks to all of my clients who make my job so fulfilling. You were my motivation to once and for all create a book that would finally give Middle American families like yours the help they have been calling out for. In particular, I want to give special thanks to Raymond and Sharlene Empeuer. Ray, I thank you for leading by example as Ray has shared with me that he too has written a book about his life experiences that encourages others to do the same. What a great way to leave a legacy not just of material wealth but of wisdom and experience. And to Sharlene, whose words ran through my mind many times as I was writing this book. When I shared my secret ambition to write a book with her I will never forget what she said. “You should write a book, you have a lot to say”. Apparently she was right.

Finally, but certainly not least, I need to express my thanks to my family. To my wife Tricia, son Nino, and daughter Katie, who patiently left me alone to write, sometimes late into the evening and on weekends. Thank you for leaving me alone long enough to complete this journey and for not ever making me feel as though I was robbing you of time that could be spent with you. I also want to say a very special thank you to my wife Tricia as she not only left me alone she truly inspired me as she does just about every day. Her belief in me has always been stronger than my belief in myself and I know in my heart of hearts I would never have accomplished half as much as I have without her love, support, and understanding. Sometimes I don't know how you do it but you are always there for me in ways I cannot begin to express.

Thank You.

Chapter 1

How The Wrong Advice Can Harm You

How To Avoid Listening To The Wrong Advice?

Where do you go for sound financial advice? Do you listen to the experts on *CNBC* or read financial publications like *The Wall Street Journal* or *Money Magazine*? Maybe you are like some of my other clients who tell me that they have a brother-in-law or someone they work with (like their boss) who seems to be doing better than they are so they take their financial cues from them. Let's face it, financial decisions get complicated real fast and most of us just don't feel like we know enough about the topic to form our own opinions so we tend to look to others when making important financial decisions. Does that sound like you? If so you may have a real problem.

If you do what everyone else is doing doesn't it make sense that you will end up like everyone else? Guess what? Everyone else is broke! Maybe more broke than you. If you don't believe me, there is an often sited study done by the U.S. Department of Labor and Statistics that states 96% of Americans are dead broke by the time they reach age 65 and only 4% are able to survive without relying on Social Security. Do you want to be in the top 4%? Then maybe you better stop listening to the bottom 96%.

But there is even more to this problem than you might realize. Even the financial experts are hurting you more than they help. Why do I say this? Are *The Wall Street Journal* and *Money Magazine* part of some evil conspiracy to keep good people like you in the poor house? Not exactly, but too often that is just what they unintentionally do. You see, most of the advice brought to you by today's media is information that is really geared toward the already wealthy and often does a disservice to us middle income folks. Wouldn't you agree that wealthy people live in a different world, with different financial rules? Can't they afford to take risks with at least some of their money? Are they concerned about getting rid of their debt so they can afford to save for their future? Do they worry about qualifying for financial aid so their children can go to college? Do they lose sleep at night wondering how they are going to put food on the table and at the same time pay for little Nino or Katie's braces? No. They just don't face the same problems and so trying to plan for our future using advice designed for the wealthy is like trying to tap in a nail to hang a picture on your wall using a sledge hammer. The recommended tools, too often, just don't fit the job.

Now, if your well-meaning friends and colleagues don't have the answers and the media's advice is not well suited for most middle income Americans then where can we turn to for sound financial advice? That is why I have written this book and it is why I devote so much time to lecturing and teaching. There are some very simple principals that if followed closely can help you easily get control of your financial life, pay off your debts quickly, start putting serious money away for emergencies and your future and have some of the better things in life.

Let me ask you some serious questions. How much debt are you in right now? Do you even know? Are you paying high interest rates of 9% or more on at least some of that debt? If you didn't have that debt over your head do you think you could be putting more money away for your future? How would you feel if you were on track to paying off all of that debt in just a few short years? If I could show you how to get your debt under control and paid off would this be one of the best books you ever read?

Now let me ask you are you happy with the amount of money you have been able to save so far? If you save as much in the next 10 years as you did in the last 10 years how are you going to feel about that? If you could learn how to put more money away for your future without you having to change your lifestyle to do it would you want to know how?

Maybe you are already a decent saver but where do you save your money? Are you happy with the returns you are getting? Is at least some of your money at risk in the stock market? How do you feel about that risk? As hard as you work for your income can you really afford to lose *ANY* money? If this book can show you how to invest your money in such a way that you were guaranteed never to have any losses yet you could still have significant gains, wouldn't you want to know how?

How about taxes? Are you happy with the amount of money you pay in taxes? With the way the government has been spending money do you think you will be paying less taxes later or more? Do you have a plan to help you pay less tax and enjoy more of your money later? This book will reveal to you some simple strategies that will help you address every one of these problems and more. So read on for the answers to your questions.

Chapter 2

Changing Times

What Used To Be True And What Is?

Did you grow up hearing this advice? Go to College. Get a *good* Job. Buy a house as soon as you can afford one. Pay it off as fast as you can. Save a little every month and you will be set for the rest of your life. Does this advice sound somewhat familiar? And who gave you that advice? Was it your Mom and Dad? Your Grandparents? Or someone else you respected and admired? Were they trying to hurt you? No, of course not. They had your best interest at heart. But what is wrong with that advice?

If you consider the source the advice made a lot of sense. After all, our parents and our grandparents lived in the same house for their entire lives. A good portion of them actually paid off their 30 year mortgages in 30 years! Many people from that generation also had only one job their entire lives. They often lived on only one income and they retired with a pension that they could count on for the rest of their lives. They had no credit card debt because almost no one used credit cards before the 1970's. And they would save a little money every month. Their parents or grandparents had experienced the Great Depression and it was drilled into them to put some money away for a rainy day and they listened. Do you know what the national savings rate was in the mid 1970's? On average people saved about 8% of their income. Wow, that is incredible by today's standards. A few other things that made that generation different was that they not only were on track to receive a reliable pension from their company but they also could expect and rely on receiving a Social Security check every month for the rest of their lives. Speaking of the rest of their lives, they did not expect that to last very long. It was almost unheard of for people to live past the age of 100! They did not live in fear of outliving their money as their Pension and Social security were guaranteed to last as long as they would and quite frankly people did not last that long.

But have things changed for this generation? Is that rock solid advice still applicable for our day? Let's take a look. Today, people almost never pay off a 30 year mortgage without refinancing. The mortgage experts tell us, that on average, people will refinance every 7 years. And if we are not prone to refinancing our loan we do tend to move every 4 to 6 years on average. Sometimes due to work relocation and other times just to upgrade. Many of us will have 3 to 7 different jobs over our life, sometimes we will get retrained and take on entirely new careers. And very few of us today actually live on one income. It often takes two people working just to make ends meet. But these are not the only differences. Here are some of the more important ones.

Today, the average family has about $16,048 in credit card debt and is paying, on average, about 15 – 20% for that debt.[1] Are credit cards a problem for most people of this generation? You bet they are.

How about savings? Are we saving enough money to be able to reach a point of financial independence? In 1970, the national savings rate was 9.6% on average[2]; do you know that it is today? It's an embarrassing 7.5% [3]as a nation we are spending more money than we make every year. Where will that leave you?
Can we at least count on our employer's pension plan to take care of us when we get old and are unable to work? No,

[1] Here's the Average American's Credit Card Debt -- and How to Get Yours Under Control. (n.d.). Retrieved from https://www.fool.com/the-ascent/credit-cards/blog/heres-the-average-americans-credit-card-debt-and-h/
[2] U.S. Personal Saving Rate, 1970-2012. (n.d.). Retrieved from http://www.hamiltonproject.org/charts/u.s._personal_saving_rate_1970-2012
[3] US Personal Savings Rate:. (n.d.). Retrieved from https://ycharts.com/indicators/us_personal_savings_rate

because our employers have phased out pensions at an alarming rate. Or at least what we used to call a pension. There used to be something called a Defined Benefit Pension Plan that would guarantee your retirement income for as long as you lived. The company you worked for would use a formula based on your income and the amount of years you worked for them to calculate how big your monthly check would be. Most importantly it was guaranteed not to run out no matter how long you lived. It is estimated that while these plans used to be the norm they are going the way of the dinosaur and only about 30,000 companies still have one. (And many of these companies are trying to get rid of them or have already begun to faze them out) What's worse is many of the companies that still offer these plans are having serious funding problems and many workers who counted on these plans and other benefits for retirement will end up receiving less money than they thought. This has already happened to steel workers, auto workers, airline workers, coal workers and so on. As if this was not bad enough when you take into account the volatile stock market, and a sluggish economy, and ad that to the fact that most of these pension plans have been under funded to begin with you have a pension system that is in serious trouble. The question arises, even if you still have a Defined Benefit Pension, will you actually be able to collect when the time comes?

There is an even bigger underlying problem that often goes unnoticed by most Middle American workers. It is more wool that has been pulled over their eyes in an attempt to divert the whole pension problem away from big business and onto whom? You guessed it, the little guy, the middle income worker. The truth of the matter is that Defined Benefit Pension Plans were an incredible program for the average worker, why? You didn't have to figure out how much of your pay you should set aside. You didn't have to worry about how to invest that money so that you would not lose it in the stock market. You did not have to figure out how to turn that money into an income stream in retirement.

You did not have to worry that you would outlive your money. All of those problems fell on your employer and the good news was that they had the resources and knowledge to figure out how to best handle all of those problems. But it was expensive and inconvenient for them and when the 401(k) was introduced, they (big business) saw it as their ticket out of a very complex, very expensive problem. Think back to that meeting where your company told you all about the great new benefit they were offering you, the 401(k).

Do you remember when your company introduced you to the 401(k) plan? They made it sound like the best thing in the world didn't they? You would now get a new tax-break that you didn't have before. They were going to help you out by matching your contributions. And you would have all of these great investments to choose from where you would make untold profits and retire with a huge savings account. But why were they really so excited about this plan? By changing from an old system, the Defined Benefit Pension Plan to the new 401(k) plan, they could now relieve themselves of all of the investment headaches, all of the responsibilities of managing your pension for you and they shifted all of those problems on to you. Now, if you didn't put enough away for your future. It's your problem. You should have saved more. If your investments don't perform well and you lose money, that's your problem, you should have done your homework and planned better. And hey, if you run out of money in retirement you can't blame us, (big business). After all we did give you a match and provide you with a plan. Is it really big businesses fault if you fail?

Do you see what they did? The took all of that expense, all of that hassle, all of that responsibility, and all of that obligation and dumped it on your lap relieving them of all future responsibility for your retirement needs. And they made it sound like they were doing you a favor. Now, if you get a little angry when you read this you should! After all how is the average working class Middle American supposed to all of a sudden become a financial planner. And do you really want to become one? My guess is if you wanted those kinds of headaches you would have left that company and started your own small business years ago. And if you do happen to be a small business owner then, yes, this responsibility has always been yours. The problem is you are too busy trying to keep your company going that you don't have time to create a retirement plan for you and your workers. So, here you are with this whole problem that you did not ask for thrown on your lap. What are you going to do about it?

What most people do is blindly under fund their future by meagerly contributing to their 401(k) plan up to the company match and they pick a few funds that their boss (who knows less than they do about investing but won't admit how much money he actually lost in the market over the last 10 years) helps them pick and then they bury their heads in the sand and use the following excuses for doing nothing about the problem. I can't put anything more away for retirement I can barely make ends meet now. I can't put anything away for retirement my company might be going out of business. I can't put anything away for retirement I have to focus on getting out of debt. Since I can't do anything now I will just do what I can and hopefully I will be able to get by on Social Security. Yikes!

First of all, I want you to know there will never be a good time to put more money away for your future and if you wait for that day to come you will miss the boat. The truth is that even if you make a modest income you will have over a million dollars pass through your hands over your working life. The question is how much of it will you keep? The answer to that question will depend much less on circumstances and much more on attitude. If you really want to change your future financial position it is most likely well within your power to do so. This book will give you many of the tools you need. But first, some of you may need a wakeup call. You will notice above that I used the word "Yikes" when referring to living on Social Security. Why? There are two reasons. Can you really live on that meager amount of income? The average Social Security check is around $1,413.08 per month or $16,956.96 per year.[4] How much income do you make now? How much of that do you need to live? Could you live on $14,400 per year? Could you live on $14,400 per year even if you managed to pay off your home and your car and all of your other debts and never make another financed purchase as long as you live? Will the cost of living go up by the time you actually retire? Will the cost of living continue to go up after you retire? If this is your plan, Yikes!

Here is reason number two why I said "Yikes" to the "I'm going to live on Social Security reasoning. Every year you get a Social Security statement projecting your earnings. It comes in your mail about 3 months before your birthday. If you are like most people you flip it open and start looking at how much you can expect to collect when you reach retirement age. Then, maybe, you glance at your income history to make sure they got your numbers right and then you file it away till next year never giving it another thought. Well, next time you get your statement, or if you have an old one lying around, I want you to actually look at the front page and read the section marked, **"About Social Securities Future".** Here is what it said on my statement last year word for word. *"In 2017 we will begin paying more in benefits than we collect in taxes. Without changes by 2041 the Social Security trust fund will be exhausted"*. Now, while that sounds bleak, the real picture is even darker. This is just what they are willing to admit and does not take into account that Medicare is in even worse trouble. According to an article in Financial Advisor Magazine, *" current benefit levels (for Social Security and Medicare) are unsustainable...By 2020, as much as 26.6% of all federal*

[4] Campbell, T. (2017, August 30). How Big Is the Average Person's Social Security Check? Retrieved from https://www.fool.com/retirement/2017/08/30/how-big-is-the-average-persons-social-security-che.aspx

income taxes would be required to sustain current Social Security and Medicare benefits for the greatly expanded population" Just think about that for a moment. If more than one out of every four dollars the government collects in taxes will soon be going to fund just these two programs, what will happen to all the other government programs? What will happen to taxes? If part of your retirement plan is to rely on Social Security "Yikes" you better think again.

My point in telling you all of this is not to scare the heck out of you but to give you a wakeup call. So, here it is in plain English. Please, do not say you were never warned. Your company is not going to take care of you. The government is not going to take care of you. Benefits will continue to be cut and taxes will continue to go up. This is not a political stand it is simple mathematics. No matter what side of the fence you are on, these are the facts. The question is what are you going to do about it? Will you bury your head in the sand and go on thinking that someone else will figure it out for you, or will you start to take responsibility for your future and have a plan. Your future does not have to be bleak but the choices you make now will determine if you will be left out in the cold or well taken care of. Another way to look at it can be summed up in this old adage, "the only difference between a crazy old man and an eccentric gentleman is money". Which one do you want to be? Do you have a plan to get there? Do you want a plan? Then read this entire book.

Chapter 3

Financial stress-relief For All

How the Middle American Worker Can Obtain True Financial Stress-Relief

I do not wish to sell you a bill of goods on which I cannot deliver. So, I feel that it is necessary to issue a bit of a disclaimer before I continue. Excuse me if I get a little philosophical in this prelude, but I want you to have a clear picture of what I am promising you before you choose whether or not to follow this advice.

I started this section with a bold promise of financial stress-relief. If you are like many Middle American families, you probably feel like financial security is really not within your reach. There seems to be just too many factors working against you. After all, as I write this book the economy is tanking. The stock market is down. And I just told you why your company and the government are not looking out for your best interest. Add to this, that the typical middle income person is shoulder deep in debt and has very little savings if any and you might be thinking financial stress-relief yeah right.

Well, in the rest of this book I will be introducing to you some core principals of wealth that if you choose to live by you will be able to get a handle on your finances and for once in your life feel like you are in control again no matter what income level you are currently at. You will no longer feel subject to the ups and downs of the stock market. You will no longer be a slave to your banker paying out 30% or more of your income to interest. And, you will also avoid to a large degree the enslavement to your Uncle Sam who tries to collect another 30% or more of your income to fund the government. You will avoid all of these enslavements by being made aware of them, more so than ever before, and I will give you alternate, legal strategies on how to avoid all of these pitfalls.[5]

Now, while that may sound like financial stress-relief to you, and it may be much better than the alternative of living a life in financial darkness, I feel obligated as the author of this book to tell you that on a deeper level I do not feel financial stress-relief is something anyone can truly obtain in the world in which we live. While we here in the U.S. live under one of the strongest nations to have ever existed, even nations such as this one have come and gone. The real truth is that everything is subject to change. Entire monetary systems have come and gone and become extinct. I tell you this not to discourage you but to help you to think outside of the box. In reality all we can do is play the game by the rules we are currently under, but if the rules change we need to change with them if we want to survive.

I also believe that to have true security you must have faith in something much more important than money. Many things that happen to us are completely out of our control and even the best financial planning could not help you evade them. So when things really go wrong sometimes having access to some money can go a long way to make you feel secure but there are other things in life that no matter how much money you have it will be of no comfort to you. If you follow my principals, I encourage you to look elsewhere for true security. I do not wish to preach to you as the point of this book is to help you better yourself financially but I will share with you that I found my truest security from my lifelong

---

[5] Pursuant to requirements imposed by the Internal Revenue Service, any tax advice contained in this communication (including any attachments) is not intended to be used, and cannot be used, for purposes of avoiding penalties imposed under the United States Internal Revenue Code or promoting, marketing or recommending to another person any tax-related matter. Please contact us if you wish to have formal written advice on this matter.

study of the Holy Bible and my personal relationship that I have forged with my creator. For me this is the only means to any real measure of security.

One Bible writer put it this way… *"Give orders to those who are rich in the present system of things not to be high-minded, and to rest their hope,* ***not*** *on uncertain riches, but on God, who furnishes us all things richly for our enjoyment."* 1Timothy 6:17

I know it may sound a little unusual for a financial author to go on about the importance of spirituality in achieving a feeling of stress-relief, but this author is well aware that we are living in a tumultuous time in history where the very fabric of our lives and the things we have put our trust in for years have been shaken. Things are not as they once were and many in the financial world are saying this is not financial planning as usual. Things are different now. While I try not to get too caught up in media hype, my 16 years experience in this industry and my lifetime study of the Bible tell me that there is only one way to proceed. One attitude to adopt. What comes around goes around in the financial world, and that translates to cycles. What goes up must come down and vice versa. The stock market does not go straight up forever and it will not go down forever. The same is true for real-estate. There will always be booms and busts as long as the world as we know it continues. However, we must also accept that the world "as we know it" may not continue forever. We are on the crux of some serious changes yet all any of us can do is speculate as to how those changes will play out. It is for this reason that I encourage you to follow the sound principals in this book. They will help you become more financially stress-relief no matter what this changing world throws at you. Beyond that I encourage you, if you are so inclined to develop a relationship with your creator as this helps no matter what your financial circumstances and it is the only path to true security.

Now I will step down from my soap box and reveal to you the key principals of financial stress-relief for the Middle American worker and how you can never have to worry about money again while enjoying your paycheck no matter how small.

Chapter 4

How to Better Manage Your Debt

Taking Back Control

I think it goes without saying that you will never feel financial stress-relief as long as you have more debt than you are comfortable with. However, just like any other *financial tool* we must remember that debt is just that a *financial tool.* When used properly it can help build empires but when abused it can be the source of much stress.

Now if you already feel like you have your debt under control then I applaud and congratulate you. You are welcome to skip this section of the book and move on to the other key principles. However, you may also want to read on as debt can sneak up on anyone at any time. Sometimes bad things happen to good people and before you know it you end up in debt. You could have an unexpected medical emergency that keeps you from working and leaves you with a pile of medical bills. Or a messy divorce where your spouse runs up all kinds of debt just for spite and your attorney bills bleed you dry on top of your other expenses. So having the skills to deal with debt may come in handy. Also, you may learn some basic strategies to help you stay on the straight and narrow. So read on if you like.

For those of you who are struggling with debt now or for those who this has been an ongoing problem this section of the book will give some great principals and strategies to help attack your debt and take back control of your financial life. So let's get started.

Stop Using Credit Cards. Period!

I know this is not a new idea for you and I also know that this is not popular medicine. However, would you agree that it is impossible for you to fill up a pail full of water when that pail is full of holes? That is exactly what you are trying to do if you are trying to get out of debt but at the same time you keep adding to it. It just won't work.

However, let me give you some good news. If you can stop using your credit cards for just a few months you will start to see your balances come down in a very short period of time. You will be encouraged by what you were able to achieve with so little effort and you will start to feel in control of your finances. If you don't believe me just try this little experiment.

Exercise: Jot down all of your debts. Not just the names of the credit cards or the major purchases but how much you owe on each one. Then add them all up. Now for some of you this may be a very painful experience in itself because you are a chicken. That's right I called you a chicken, cluck, cluck. You don't even know how much you owe, and you are afraid to look. Do it! You cannot grow if you are unwilling to face your fears. Now, I want you to cut up ALL of your credit cards. (Don't close the accounts as this will hurt your credit score.) You can always call them up and have them issue you a new one but let's try and avoid it for now. Give yourself a 4 month reprieve from using your credit cards. At the end of the 4 months, after making 4 months of your usual payments, add up all of your balances again and see how much you owe. You will be amazed at how much you will be able to pay off in that short period of time. Even if all you do is pay your minimums you will be well on your way to a great start in gaining control over your finances.

Some of you may be saying to yourself but I can't stop using my credit cards because…

(Fill in your excuse here)

____.

Yeah, I know it may take some adjustments but it can be done. I have done it. I have clients that have done it. Heck, 35 years ago before they had so many credit cards how did people do it? Why not ask someone who lived back then? It is possible to live without credit cards.

Now, if you use credit cards for online purchases or booking travel most of those same companies will accept debit cards. And if you are concerned with using debit cards for security reasons, I am sure if you make your plans ahead of time you can usually pay by check through the mail. If you are disciplined, you can open a credit card account just for these types of purchases but then again if you were disciplined that would not really be necessary would it? My advice is stop using your credit cards, and stop adding to your debt until you can get it paid off.

But what if an emergency comes up like your car breaks down or your water heater goes out? First of all make sure it is really an emergency. One of my clients recently complained to me that they had to kick in unexpected money for a catered graduation party for their step-kid from a former marriage. That is not an emergency. That was a choice. (It may not have felt like much of a choice at the time, but it was a choice) You could always admit that you don't have money for that in your budget, and choose not to kick in this time, couldn't you?

Sure, you would feel like a heel but you would be a heel that could pay their bills on time. Secondly, if it really is an unavoidable emergency like fixing your car so you can get to work the next day, and the only way you can pay for it is on credit then fine go ahead and charge it. But remember, these are generally not the types of purchases that get us in trouble. It is usually the little day to day things like charging clothing, dinners out or vacations that we can't afford that cause the real problems.

So, after you try the above exercise do it again and again and stop using those cards. If you get nothing else from this book this may be the single most powerful strategy you can embrace. Try it for a while and you will thank me when you start to feel control and peace of mind again. Here are some other things you can do that will help you enjoy the freedom of a pay as you go "cash only" lifestyle.

Track Your Spending

I don't know who said it first, but this is one of Bob Parsons, CEO of GoDaddy.com's rules to live by,

"Measure everything of significance. Everything that is measured and watched improves."

This is an incredibly profound statement, and it is really true. I want to give you a quick example of just how true this principal is. I am a life time member of a well know weight management program. Since I have been in this program I have lost 60 pounds, and managed to keep that weight off now for a little over 4 years. I am sure you would agree that this is a very positive success story, and a true one. But how did I do it?

One of the simplest things I learned is that to lose weight you need to pay attention to and track how much you eat every day. When I first started doing this I learned something interesting about my eating habits. I knew I was eating more than I should but I did not realize how much harm I was really doing. I used to work really late and sometimes found myself coming home at 11:00 at night. By this time in the evening I was hungry and felt like I deserved a little late night snack for all of my hard work so I would stop at a popular fast food taco place on the way home. I would order my favorite 3 or 4 items and eat them in front of the TV as I unwound from a very busy day. Once I started tracking my food intake I looked up those items, and found out that I had been unknowingly consuming one and a half days' worth of food in just that one sitting. I was shocked! I knew my late night snacks were bad but not that bad. I learned a valuable lesson. Not paying attention to what you are doing can get you into a lot of trouble. Once I started tracking my food intake I learned some other valuable lessons too.

I learned that there were items for sale at the taco place that had far less calories than I thought. So by just making some small pain free adjustments I could actually still eat at my favorite taco place while losing weight. It was like having my cake and eating it too. Pardon the expression.

Tracking your money works exactly the same way. If you pay a little closer attention to where your money is going you may find some places you are spending money that are incredibly wasteful and really not worth it to you. (You tend to realize these more quickly when you are trying to live only on the cash you have, another reason why stopping all charges is so important) I had a client once that started tracking his expenses and realized he was spending $97 per month on going out for coffee every day at his office. Instead his very smart wife told him she would buy him a special coffee maker that brewed gourmet coffee one cup at a time. The machine cost a one-time purchase of $30 and the coffee for the machine cost about $10 per month. Add in some sugar and creamer that he kept in his office and he went from spending $97 per month down to spending about $15.00 per month saving him $82.00 per month. Wow. He now saves that $82 per month in his retirement account. If he earns just 8% interest over the next 25 years he will have $78,504, and he still has his afternoon coffee every day! Could there be some things in your budget that you could adjust? Here is how you find out.

Exercise: For one month, keep track of everything you spend. Get your whole family involved. One way you can do this would be to save every receipt from every purchase you make no matter how small. Another way would be to make all of your purchases on a debit card for one month. Either way you choose, once you have all of your data gathered put it into categories like dinners out, entertainment, dry cleaning, groceries, etc.… Now you will be able to see exactly where all of your money is going and what can be adjusted.

You don't have to do this exercise every month but it might not be a bad idea to repeat it now and again to see what kind of wasteful spending habits might have crept in. Remember, too, that the point of this exercise is not to see how you can squeeze every penny out of your budget, but you are looking for areas you are spending money that really are not that important to you. If you can find just one or two of these wasteful habits and re-direct that money somewhere smarter you can really make a huge difference without having to give up something you enjoy spending your money on. On the other hand, if you happen to be at a stage of life right now where you are really struggling then maybe you need to be a little harsher with your cutbacks. However, life tends to change quite often and once you master the skills in this book, money will not be as big of a problem for very long. So, even if you have to make some drastic cut backs, remember, they are only temporary.

Another thing I recommend you do is to start a budget. Now don't get me wrong. For the most part, a budget is about as useful as a diet. No one ever sticks to one so you really have to think of it as more of a spending plan than a budget. I personally use a really great system to help me track every penny that goes through my accounts. In fact, I personally update it every Friday so if you ask me on a Friday how much money I have socked away for any given expense I can tell you. Another thing I like about using a tracking system is I can save money for a specific goal without having to open up a separate account. For example most people are familiar with the old Vacation Club, or Holiday Club accounts at your local savings and loan. These plans work because they are automated and also because they take that money and physically move it to another account out of your reach. I love this idea, as it works great against our human tendency to want to spend money we shouldn't, and thinking we will make it up later when in reality we never do. My budget software lets me do the same thing without having to actually physically move the money. I can have one checking account, but break it up into as many small sub accounts as I want and this helps me put money away for things I might need.

For example, in one of my sub accounts I am saving for a new computer for my office. Every time I get paid, I distribute my money into all of the sub accounts that I created. The one for my computer gets $100 per month from my paycheck. I currently have $800 saved in that sub account that I know I can't touch because it is for my computer. Now when I go to buy that computer I can write a check instead of put it on a credit card helping me to stay out of debt. You can and should even create sub accounts for unexpected things like when the car breaks down. This one is harder to plan for but let's say an average car repair is $600 for your car and your car breaks down or needs some major maintenance about once per year. You could put $50 per month into your auto maintenance sub account. Then, when your car breaks down, you won't have to reach for your credit card.

This may sound like a lot of work but it really is not as bad as you think. You may have to spend one or two days on a weekend setting it up, but after that much of the process can be automated. Your computer may even have come with a program capable of doing this but I am no techie and have found that most programs are a little more complicated than I want. So instead I use a program that is ultra-simple. If you want to check it out you can download it for free and try it out for 3 months before you decide if you want to buy it, and then it is only $30.00. I make nothing on this product, and I am not an affiliate for them but I did put a link to their site here: http://www.snowmintcs.com/ or you can use any other budget tracking app or program that is made for us old schoolers that you may want to use. This is the program that I use. But just make sure you use something. It's just like a diet. If I stop tracking what I eat, I tend to eat a lot more. But when I write it down I am more in control. The same is true with spending.

As my weight management coach once said, *" We would all love to just go through life without a care in the world, never balancing our check book or being restricted in anyway, but if we did that where would that leave us?"* --*Tonya.*

Keeping track of what you are doing is a necessary evil. You may not like it but it goes a long way toward getting you to your goals.

Create a Debt Pay Down Plan

If you are like many of my clients, getting out of debt might be listed at the top of your financial goal list. In fact, for many of my clients, they can't see past this goal as it has become their most pressing financial problem. They feel as if their debt is just growing and growing month after month, year after year and if they don't get a handle on it they will drown in it. Does that sound like you? I hope not, but have no fear even if you are feeling that downhearted about your debt there is hope and I am about to show you how to shed some light on that hope and make it crystal clear.

If debt is a major problem for you then you need to create a debt pay down plan. What is a debt pay down plan you may ask? Simply put it is a written plan showing exactly how and when you will get out of debt. I have found that the easiest way to do this is to find an online calculator and plug in your numbers. I know of a website that will let you run all kinds of scenarios.

You can check it out at https://www.dinkytown.net.

When you visit the site, just find a tab marked calculators. However, if crunching numbers is not your thing, that's fine, just get some help. If you live in my area, this is a free service that I offer because I own a really great software system that can knock this out in just minutes.

Here is what you will need to enter. Your balance (how much you owe today on each debt) your interest rate (per year) and what you actually pay each month. With just these few pieces of information the software will compute how long it will take you to pay off your debts. My software will even create a month by month plan showing you exactly how much to pay to each debt to optimize your plan.

Here is what you will learn. In most cases you will see that you can pay off your debts a lot sooner than you thought if you just stick to a plan and as I said before, **stop using credit cards, period**. While figuring out how much you owe may seem a bit scary to face, to some, knowing that you can get out of debt in your lifetime and get your life back can be a very liberating experience. I have done this for hundreds of clients and it is as if I can actually see the weight being lifted off their shoulders. They look like they are leaving my office 50lbs lighter. (I love when that happens)

There is one more reason why you must have a written **Debt Pay down plan…**

Credit Card Companies Are Sneaky

That's right I said it. Credit cards companies are sneaky, and they want you to be in debt to them as long as humanly possible. They are not your friend. They know that the longer it takes you to pay off that debt the more interest they will collect from you. So, here is what they do and how you can avoid their trap.

Have you ever heard this advice before, "always pay a little more than the minimum"? Clients come into my office all the time telling me how proud they are that they never pay minimums. Well, of course it is better to pay more than the minimum but actually not much better. Here is why just paying more than the minimums does not work.

The credit card companies know that you are likely to try and pay a little more than the minimum. So, to stretch your debt out longer, they lower your minimum every month. This process makes it nearly impossible to pay off your credit cards in your lifetime using that strategy. In fact the two worst things you could ever do if you are trying to get out of credit card debt for good is 1) Continue using your credit cards and 2) make payments that are based on your minimum due.

Paying a little more than the minimum simply just does not work. Let's look at a quick example. Let's say you have a credit card balance of $10,000 and your minimum payment is $200 and your interest rate is 15.99%. If you pay only the minimum guess how long it will take you to pay off that debt? **39 years and 3 months**, Ouch! But what if you paid a little extra like $10 per month? Then, it would only take you **34 years and 11months**. Well, that is better but not by much. Why? Because you were basing your payment on the minimum and the credit card company keeps lowering it to stretch out your payment. Now let's look what would happen if you had a written debt pay down plan and you paid a level

$210.00 per month, every month no matter what the minimum on your card said. You would be out of debt in just **6 years and 5 months. Wow!** And you could do that without having to spend any more money than you are spending right now.

You only need to change two things. 1) Stop using credit cards and adding to your debt and 2) Have a plan to get them paid off that ignores the minimums. (Don't get me wrong, you still have to always make sure you are paying at least what they are billing you or you will have to pay late fees and higher interest rates. But as a rule, you don't want to base your payment amount on what they are asking you for) Remember, the credit cards are setting you up for failure because when you fail they win.

Now we're going to talk about something that really blows my clients minds. I want you to do something very unconventional…

Stop Paying That Little Bit Extra To All Of Your Credit Cards

I already told you the first reason why paying a little extra to your credit card each month does not work. Now, I am going to show you why doing this on every card are not likely to get you out of debt sooner.

Here is what I find that most people do… Are you guilty of this? Most of my clients get their credit card bills and if they ask for $97 they pay $100 or if they ask for $35 they pay $50. Because they are always paying a little more than asked they feel like they are at least keeping their debts in check, but nothing could be further from the truth.

For one thing, I ask these same clients who are trying to get out of debt but seem to be getting nowhere if they are still using credit cards. Can you guess what most of them say? If they are honest, they will tell me that they are still using them. Or they will tell me that they are *trying* not to. As if someone is physically dragging them to the store, and insisting they pay with credit.

What is happening is a vicious cycle. They are trying to do what is right by paying a little extra each month but they can't afford to buy what they need with cash because they have no money left. And they have no money left because they are paying more than they even realize to their debt. Can you see how this can create a vicious cycle?

But how do you break this cycle? Simple. Just follow the steps I have outline above and then add one more.

1) Stop using credit (at least for a while)
2) Create a debt pay down plan (put it all in writing)

And now step 3. Stop paying that little bit extra on all of your credit cards, and instead, take back control of that money and decide how to use it towards your best advantage.

Let me give you a small example. Let's look at the typical family with a heavy debt load. Their payments often look something like this...

Card	Balance Due	Minimum	Actual Payment	Difference
Visa	$4,500	$90	$100	$10
Master Card	$3,500	$70	$100	$30
Visa #2	$1,900	$38	$50	$12
Home Depot	$3,800	$76	$100	$24
Clothing Card	$800	$16	$80	$64
Car Loan	$13,000	$272	$300	$28
Home Equity	$9,800	$65	$200	$135
Totals	$37,800	$627	$930	$303

Does this remind you of anyone? Well, what is this family doing? They are paying extra on all of their debts hoping that their debt will not get away from them. They have probably never totaled up their debts the way I have and they don't know how much they actually owe because they are chicken. But is this strategy working for them? What do you think? If you looked at their balances 6 months from now, would you expect to find more or less debt than you see here? I can tell you it is almost always going to be more. That's because they have not followed rules one and two. But let's look at what we can accomplish by using rule number three.

Here is what I have learned. Once you are armed with the above information, you can go down one of two roads. You can keep charging and keep trying to pay off that little bit extra only to end up in a bankruptcy attorney's office someday. Not a great choice. Or you can stop charging, create a written pay down plan and use the money we just "found" to fund some of your other financial goals.

How far does $303 per month go in your household? Could you perhaps add that money back into your budget so that you would have more cash to spend? Would that make giving up the use of your credit cards a little easier? With $303 per month to spend do you think you might be able to start that emergency fund that you have been meaning to start? Could you perhaps apply some of that money to your debt pay down plan in a more organized way?

I have found that helping families to see that they are mindlessly giving that money to their bills before taking care of some of their own basic needs can be very empowering. It can give you back a little control of your own money.

But how you decide to use this money can make a huge difference in your life. So think carefully…

Think about this. If you could save that $303 a month for one whole year how much would you have in the bank? $3,636! And that is without earning any interest. How much could you have in just 5 years? $18,180. How secure would you feel if you had that much money in your emergency fund right now? Would you be under less stress?

By the way if you save $303 a month for just 20 years and earn a paltry 5% return you would have $125,062 saved!

As you can see that $303 dollars extra this family is paying towards their debt each month is costing them way more than $303. They are giving up on $125,062 of retirement savings that they could have had without having to change their lifestyle. How much money are you willing to give up to the bank?

Think about it. Even if they never got that debt paid down and they still ended up owing the same $37,800 because they spun their wheels paying down debt and charging it up again for the same 20 years wouldn't they be better off if they saved that $303. They would be in a position to pay off all of their debt and still have $87,262 left! ($125,062 saved - $37,800 of debt = $87,262 left over)

Now I'm going to give you a little tip that will make sure you stick to your debt pay down plan....

Always Pay Off Your Smallest Debts First!

The order you should pay off your debts should be based on paying down the smallest debt you have first. For example, let's say you just completed step 3 and you found out you have $303 and your primary goal is to get out of debt. You would take that full $303 and apply it to your smallest debt each month. Why?

Because in the above example their smallest debt was an $800 clothing bill and if they used this method they would have that debt completely wiped out in under 3 months. With the clothing bill gone they can now take the $16 they were paying to the clothing bill and add it to the $303 and so they could pay an extra $319 to their next smallest bill.

In this example they would pay that $319 plus the normal minimum payment of $38.00 to their Visa #2 that they owe $1,900 on. How fast could that bill be paid off? They would have that bill paid in about 5 months.

Do you see the snowball effect happening here? In just 8 months they would have knocked out two debts and have freed up a lot of cash per month that could be applied to their next smallest debt and so on.

This is one of the fastest and most effective ways to pay down your debt and it works great because it incorporates human nature. After all, it was human nature that got you into debt why not use it to help get you out?

If you go on a diet and eat a poached egg and dry toast for breakfast and dry tuna over a bed of lettuce every day for lunch and you skip dinner and you do this for a whole week and you get on the scale after that week and you lost nothing, what are you **not** going to be doing next week? Dieting, that's what!

Our human nature craves instant satisfaction. That is why most of us end up in debt to begin with. So if we create a debt pay down plan and we don't see any positive results, how long are we going to stick with that plan?

Now, some of you math wiz's are asking yourself, "shouldn't you pay off the debt with the highest interest rate first?" I say sure, if you want to be in debt for the rest of your life. After all, how well has that advice served you thus far? That is what all the other gurus suggest yet people read their books and articles and more people are struggling with debt than ever before. Besides, I have done the math for clients hundreds of times and just for fun I always run a comparison. I run the numbers paying down your smallest debt first and then I run it paying down the highest interest rate first and guess what? I have never found a situation where the clients would get out of debt one month faster paying down the highest interest rate first. That is not to say that you might be able to trim a month or two off your plan in some circumstances. But trust me; those circumstances are few and far between.

So, pay off your smallest debt first and enjoy the snowball effect that you will create. You will have several debts paid off in no time.

Now let's wrap up this debt problem once and for all so we can move on to more exciting financial issues…

Your Debt Does Not Live In A Vacuum!

So far we learned 3 important steps to getting and staying out of debt and one tip that makes it go much smoother and helps you stay on track. So let's review…

Step One) Stop Using Your Credit Cards
(Or borrowing period) At least
Until you get this under control.

Step Two) Create a debt pay down plan
(Put it all in writing)

Step Three) Stop paying that little bit extra

Final Tip: Pay off your debts in the order of smallest to largest so you can experience some quick success and stick to your plan.

Bonus Tip: Don't sweat it if you mess up! Just start over. You will still be light years ahead of how most people are coping with their debt and you will end up paying yours off decades earlier even if you have a few setbacks along the way. Expect some

setbacks and you won't be disappointed.
Just don't give up. When you quit, you fail.
And things only get worse.

So, these are the basics all summed up for you. And I really hope this helps you get your finances on track to where you want to be. But that brings me to an interesting point, **where do you want to be?**

Many people seek out my help because they want to get a handle on their debt. They are so focused on getting out of debt that it becomes their number one financial goal.

But, I often ask why do you want to get out of debt? After all getting a handle on your debt is certainly a good idea but is it really your top financial goal? Have you ever asked yourself, **"Then what?"**

Let's say you magically got out of debt today and now you have all of this extra cash flow in your life, what would you do with it?

Would you go on vacation? Would you buy a new TV? A new car? Why do you want to get out of debt?

What are all of those payments holding you back from doing?

If you were debt free tomorrow, would you save some of your money in an emergency fund so that you would never have to go back into debt? And so would you feel more financial stress-relief?

Would you put some money away for your children's education? Would you start a retirement plan so that you could have enough money saved to actually stop working some day?

Would you buy some of the insurance plans that you know you need to protect yourself and your family but didn't think you could afford because of all of your debt payments?

These are some important questions aren't they? You see, your financial concerns won't go away just because your debt is paid. In fact your debt is only one piece of the financial puzzle.

I recently met with a 65 year old man who had spent his whole life listening to the advice of a well know get out of debt guru. He came to one of my workshops and took me up on an offer to meet with him for a free consultation. What I found out was this man did a fantastic job of staying out of debt. His condo was paid for; he had no credit card debt, and no car loans. He owed nothing. I congratulated him on this as most of my clients are not so fortunate. However, when I was reviewing his assets he had only saved about $10,000 over his entire life! He was now 65 years old and still working. I imagine he will be working as long as they let him as the only money he will have to live on is Social Security and that is not going to afford him much of a lifestyle. Was this man a financial success? You tell me. Is this what you want for your future?

I tell you this story because I want to encourage you to think beyond your debt. Your debt does not live in a vacuum. It should not be your **ONLY** financial goal. Think beyond it even if you are struggling with it and remember if you wait until you pay everything off before you learn how to save money it may just be too late.

Chapter 5

How To Protect Yourself And Your Family The Right Way

Protect Yourself And Your Family

Most people think about insurance as a cost item or an expense and so they tend to get the least they have to so they can get by. And they are right in that there is no need to spend more money than necessary on insurance plans. In fact sometimes paying into too many unnecessary insurance plans can drain your budget so deeply that there is no money left to save or invest for your future. This would not be a good use of a Middle American person's income. After all there is only so much money to go around.

However, what if things go wrong? What if your house burns down, or you crash the car, or you need an expensive operation due to a sudden change in your health? What if you are unable to work due to an illness and your income stops for 6 months or a year or more? What if you pass away suddenly and leave your family one income short of paying the bills? What do you want to happen to them?

While insurance can be expensive it is no doubt necessary. But what plans do you really need and when is it overkill? I want to spend a little time talking about how you can cut down your insurance costs by self-insuring, as well as what insurance plans are critical and which ones you can live without.

But before we get into all of that, you need to keep in mind that insurance is more than a necessary evil. It is an incredible tool. If used properly it can help your financial plan stay on track no matter what. Think about this. If you went to the best financial planner in the world and you were able to set up a great savings and investment plan that would allow you to meet all of your goals but then you got sick or injured and could no longer work, or you needed an expensive operation that drained all of your savings, what would become of your plan? The best financial plan in the world without insurance is a very weak plan indeed. So this is a very important topic, let's get started…

Self-Insure Whenever Practical

Wealthy people have understood and used the concept of self-insurance for hundreds of years, but I am not writing this book for the wealthy, so how does this affect the rest of us? It affects all of us, because wealthy or not we can still understand and use this important principal. Here are the basic ideas.

Self-insuring is when you can set aside enough money to cover the risk yourself instead of paying money to an insurance company to cover the risk. Now while this sounds simple enough you cannot just declare, "Ok that sounds great I'll just self-insure" you first have to make sure you actually have enough money to protect yourself and your family from the inherent risk.

By the way, some people say insurance is just a gamble. This is not really true. Here is the difference.

The very act of gambling creates a risk where there was none before. Insuring on the other hand protects you from a risk that already exists.

The reality is that there are many risks of many things that can go wrong. We can't protect ourselves from all of them but we need to examine which ones we can self-insure against, which ones we can gamble won't happen to us and which ones we need to rely on insurance companies for.

So here is a practical example of self-insuring that you may want to look into for your own situation. How many years have you been driving? Let's say you have been a driver for 20 years (for our example). Now how many times have you crashed your car and had to rely on your Car Insurance to reimburse you? Let's say 3 times. Each time you crashed your car how much did you have to shell out of your pocket to meet the insurance company's deductible. Let's say you had a deductible of $500. So in this example you self-insured $500 per accident and the insurance company picked up the rest of the tab.

I bet you didn't know you were already using this strategy did you? Wow! You must be pretty smart. Maybe you don't need this book after all. Oh, but wait a minute. What if you had decided to self-insure for $1000 instead of only $500?

But then I would have had to pay a total of $3,000 out of pocket for my 3 accidents instead of only $1,500 that's no good, I don't like it, you say.

True, however there is a flip side to this math problem. What would have happened to your insurance premium when you had raised your deductible? You would have paid less to the insurance company because you agreed to take on more of the risk and that put them less at risk right? So how much money would you have saved? Let's say that upping your deductible saved you $200 per year and you paid this smaller premium for 20 years. That means you would have paid $4,000 less to the insurance company and only been on the hook for $1,500 more in deductibles. So how far ahead would you be? $4,000 premium savings - $1,500 of additional deductibles paid = $2,500.

Now you might say $2,500 is not that much money over 20 years but isn't it better off in your pocket than in the insurance companies. Unless of course you like donating money to insurance companies and in that case I have set up a special beneficiary fund that you are welcome to contribute to. Just call me and I will tell you where to send the check.

But seriously, this is just one example. What if you did the same thing with your homeowners insurance and your health insurance and even your disability insurance?

The strategy is simply this, review all of your insurance plans and find out how much money you can save, not by dropping these important insurances, but by increasing your deductibles just a little bit on each plan.

Now you might also think that increasing your deductibles when you don't have the extra $500 or so in the bank to actually cover the risk could actually put you in more financial danger than this is worth. And this is true to a degree so you must weigh out your options carefully and you may want to discuss this with an advisor before you make any drastic moves. Also, keep this in mind. Is it possible that the reason you don't have the $500 or so in the bank to ne able to self-insure is because you are paying more than necessary to your insurance companies. It can be a real catch 22 or a vicious cycle.

One last point on this and then we will move on. For this strategy to actually help you must take the money that you are saving and put it in some sort of savings vehicle. This way, once you have saved up enough to cover the additional risk, you will truly be self-insured. You will have the cash to cover the need if it arises and you will still have the cash if the need does not arise, plus the interest that money will earn.

Also, later on in this book we will be talking more about how to establish emergency funds that you can access so self-insuring won't seem that far-fetched after you have a few thousand dollars or more in accessible money in your own savings plan and later on I will be explaining how this is easier to accomplish than you might have realized. So, let's move on…

What You Need And What You Can Live Without

As I mentioned at the onset of this section some insurance plans are almost crucial to financial security and others are more of a waste of money so let's talk about some of the ones that waste your money so you can get rid of them and get the insurance plans that you and your family really need.

The Losers

The first type of plan I want to mention are warranty plans. You know the ones when you buy that expensive TV, computer, kitchen appliance or electronic device they always try and sell you on the warranty. Almost all of these are a complete waste of money and here is how you can tell. As a rule for an insurance plan to be considered valuable it should provide benefits at a cost of pennies compared to dollars. In other words to be considered valid you should plunk down a few pennies compared to the dollars they will reimburse you if you actually make a claim. With warranty plans the ratio is often way off balance. For example you might pay an extra $100 to cover a $500 item. You are shelling out about 20% of the cost of the item to insure that same item. That is an astronomically high ratio. This equates to spending one dollar to cover a five dollar risk. If it were truly valuable to you it should cost much less. The truth of the matter is the insurer knows that for every 20 people who buy these plans only one will ever make a claim that costs them money. Others may make a claim but not have all of their paperwork. Others still may not have the original packaging. (Do you have the box your TV came in?) Others will make a claim but find out that the defect they are inquiring about is not covered. (The "oh you have one of those", excuse) You see your likelihood of ever getting any money out of them is so slim and they know that even if they do have to pay out now and then they will end up very profitable off of your money at the end of the day. So, don't do it.

In fact, the next time you are tempted to buy an extended warranty why not take the money it would have cost you and put it in your savings plan. If you do this you will likely have more than enough money to cover the once in a blue moon repairs that come your way. (And probably a whole lot of cash left over).

I once reviewed an automobile extended warranty plan for one of my clients and she was paying nearly $100 per month. When you read the fine print there was a $300 deductible for major repairs and a cap of $1,200 total that the company would pay. I explained to her that if she were to have a $1,500 repair on her car after one year of being in the plan she would have paid $1,200 in premium and received back her same $1,200. In essence she would have given this company an interest free loan for the year and the most she could get back from them was one year's premium. What if she paid in for 5 years? The company would be way ahead as they had placed a limit on her plan to make sure they were never on the hook for more than one year of her premium. In fact if she put that money away for just 5 years instead not only would she be able to cover anything that could ever go wrong with her car but she would have enough in the bank to replace the car with another used vehicle. This was definitely a risk she would have been better off to self-insure. The bottom line is stay away from Extended Warranties.

The next type of insurance plan that I encourage you to stay away from is accident only plans or accidental death and dismemberment plans. These plans will pay you a benefit if you have an accident. For example, you might have a free accident plan from your credit union for $1,000 and then they call you on the phone or mail you an offer to increase your coverage to $25,000, $50,000 or even $100,000. These plans are very inexpensive or at least they seem to be but here is the catch. They will only pay if you die in an accident or you are dismembered. So if you have a heart attack, a stroke, get cancer or some other type of illness you get NOTHING. What really bothers me about these plans is many middle income families have these types of plans and so they figure their families will be fine if something happens to them but in reality in most cases you will just pay and pay and never collect. It troubles me that these companies knowingly give people a false sense of security. Here is the really sad part. Often for just a little bit more per month you could have an actual insurance plan that will protect your family whether you die from an accident or a health related cause. This would be a much better option and we will talk more about that in the section on the winners.

Another loser plan is cancer insurance. These plans capitalize on the fact that so many people have lost a family member to cancer and know what kind of financial hardship that can bring. Also, you don't have to die to collect all you have to do is be diagnosed with a life threatening cancer. So many people buy these because they figure that cancer runs in the family and it could happen to them. The idea itself is not terrible. Cancer can bring about many financial hardships and the money would certainly come at a much needed time. However, I have two problems with cancer plans. One is most people who own these plans have huge gaps in other areas of insurance that are more important and many times they may end up with way too little life, disability or health insurance but they are covered if they have cancer. This is just poor planning. But in most cases it happened because no one has pointed out that this insurance premium could be better used to protect them from a wider range of problems. My second problem with these plans is they are basically obsolete as a better option has been introduced to the market called a Critical Illness Plan. Critical Illness Plans not only cover cancer but they cover other major illnesses like heart attack, stroke, loss of hearing or sight, etc.... These Critical Illness plans are much more effective than a Cancer policy and cancer is still covered. However, I would not even recommend these plans unless your other more important winner coverage's are in place.

One last group of plans you may want to be leery of are the accident plans they sell as an optional coverage you can apply for at work. Not all optional coverage's offered through employers are bad but most of these accident type plans are a waste of money. The plans I am not fond of are the ones that pay you a monthly benefit if you are out of work due to an accident or if you are in the hospital they will pay you $100 per day and so forth. These plans are based mostly on the premise that they will ONLY pay you a benefit if your situation was caused by an accident or if you are staying over in the hospital. The money you pay for these plans can be better used to buy the winner plans that I will talk about in a moment.

The basic recurring problem that I find with most Middle American families is that they buy one plan from the guy at the bank another from their mortgage company and another from their employer and then another plan from something they saw in a magazine or from an association they belong to. The end result is a hodge-podge of insurance plans that leave huge holes in the protection portfolio. In most cases they could have given their family iron clad protection for the same money they are spending if someone would just have reviewed their plans and made some minor corrections and explanations. Now, let's talk about the insurance plans that you can NOT do without and what is the best way to buy them.

The Winners

Most of the winner plans are probably obvious to you already so I won't spend a lot of time on this. The thing to keep in mind is everyone's situation is different so I will be careful not to make any blanket statements like everyone needs Auto insurance. If you don't drive a car you don't need it. The simple point here is it is all relative to your particular situation so let me list off the obvious and then get a little more detailed on some things you may not have thought about.

If you have a car, you must have Auto insurance. But, self-insure as much as you can afford, as I talked about earlier. If you own a home, you must have Homeowners insurance. But again self-insure as much as you can. If you can fog a mirror, then you need Health Insurance. Now many people are running around with no health insurance hoping they will never need it because their job does not offer it or they feel they cannot afford it. However, consider this. If you get serious about your financial future and you create a long term financial plan and you start saving for your goals and then you need an operation, what will happen to your financial plan? Won't it all go out the window? Is that what you want? Think about the damage just one emergency surgery can do to the best financial plan. I had one client that I recommended buy some health insurance and he decided to take his chances. He called me 3 weeks later and told me that he had to have emergency Gall Bladder surgery and it cost him $30,000. He didn't have $30,000 so now he was in debt to the hospital. There went his plan out the window.

The good news here is you can self-insure a large part of this risk. You don't need to get the most expensive plan they offer and you can cut your costs considerably. You will want to look for a plan with a high deductible. Again, you may be saying to yourself "but with a high deductible won't I end up paying for insurance and then still having to pay when I go to the doctor?" Yes! But you will have plenty of money to pay the doctor because of all the money you saved in insurance premiums. For example suppose a $500 deductible plan charged you $400 per month and a $5,000 deductible plan charged you only $250 per month. You would be saving $150 per month. If you saved that $150 in just one year you could self-insure the risk with your savings account of $1,800. If you did this for 5 years you would have $9,000 in your medical savings account and you could increase your deductible and save even more money. Of course I am assuming that you never go to the doctor in those 5 years but even if you did go and paid for it out of your savings do you see how you could get ahead in a very short period of time?

Remember, that the key for this to work is that you must save the difference if you can. But even if you cannot afford to save the difference wouldn't you be better off with a $5,000 or even a $10,000 deductible plan than having no insurance at all? Do you want to be the guy on the gurney they ship back out to the county hospital as soon as you're stable because you don't have any insurance? Or, do you want the best care money can buy? If you are running around with no insurance you owe it to yourself and your family to look into a high deductible plan as soon as possible, before you need it and even before you start your financial plan. (Or better yet, use this as your first step to financial stress-relief)

Now, here is another must have insurance that you may not have given much thought to in the past but you should. If you had a machine that could produce hundred dollar bills and you had no way to fix it if it broke, and someone offered you an insurance policy on that machine that only cost a fraction of the money that the machine could produce for you would you buy that policy? You would no doubt insure such a wonderful machine! Well that machine is you and your ability to produce a paycheck. Over your lifetime you will produce at least $1,000,000 if you earn around $25,000 per year or more and work an average work life. Isn't your ability to produce an income worth insuring? If you became sick or got injured and were suddenly unable to work for a long period of time, how would you pay the bills? How long would your savings last you? For most people the answer is not long at all. Most of us live paycheck to paycheck and have no real way to handle such a financial tragedy.

What you need then is Disability insurance. Now you may have some through work but in most cases even if they give you disability insurance it is a real good idea to review it from time to time. Many plans only cover a fraction of your income and that fraction may be taxable. If you think it would be hard to live on a fraction of your paycheck how hard would it be to live on say 50% of your paycheck LESS taxes? Also, many plans sold through work are accident only so read the fine print or have a trusted advisor review your work plan with you to make sure you are really protected.

You don't want to find out you were underinsured when you are trying to make a claim do you? You want to know where you stand right now to make sure you have all your ducks in a row. (And if you happen to have one of those insurance plans with a duck on it there is a good chance that all you have is accident protection. So make sure you read the fine print or find someone who can help you.) By the way if you are one of those "it's not going to happen to me people", the statistics on this are staggering. On average, a disability lasting 90 days or more is likely to happen to one out of every three people. This is an insurance you will most likely use at some point in your life, so make sure you have as much as they will let you buy and that you can afford. You can use the self-insuring method to cut the cost on these plans as well by lengthening the elimination period and shortening the benefit period. This is definitely something you want to take a careful look at with your disability agent or a trusted advisor.

Now, if you are reading this book and you are at or near retirement then you probably don't need disability insurance as your income is not dependent on you being able to get out of bed and go to work every morning. However, as soon as your need for disability goes away you will be plagued with an equally inherent risk. The risk of having your health robbed from you and your lifestyle totally disrupted. What I am talking about is Long Term Care insurance. The problem is that when you are older and you experience a debilitating change in your health and you can no longer take care of yourself, you may get to the point where you need assistance in your home or in a home. I know you are probably thinking that you never want to be in that situation but the sad reality is that this exact situation will happen to one out of two adults 65 or older before they pass away for a period of about 2 to 3 years on average. The cost of this care currently runs about $130 per day in my part of the country but it is going up every year faster than the rate of inflation. At $130 per day that comes to a cost of $3,900 per month or $46,800 per year. Where will you get that kind of money when your health changes? These costs are currently not covered by Medicare and if you think Medicaid will pay, the rules get stricter every year and they already require you to practically spend down your last penny before they pay dime one. There are ways to do some Medicaid planning to protect some of your assets but most of the time this means giving up control or gifting your money out of your estate. If you don't have any money to worry about then you should be fine as you *will* qualify for Medicaid as soon as you spend down what you do have. If you have lots of money then you can self-insure and you are probably not reading my book as I did not write it for you. So, go back to checking on your stocks, or polishing your Yacht, or doing something useful with your time. If you are the Middle American worker that I did write the book for, chances are your lifetime of hard work will be wiped out unless you plan for this important risk. I would hate to see that happen. So, talk with your advisor and ask him/her about how to set up some protection for Long Term Care. If he/she is smart they can even show you ways to protect yourself without having to pay a monthly premium using something called an Asset Based Long Term Care Plan.

The last winner insurance I want to talk about is life insurance. Who needs it? **Only people who love other people.** If you don't care much about your spouse and your kids or you have no one or no charity in your life that you really care about then you don't need life insurance and you are probably a very unhappy human being. But, if you have someone or some organization that you care about then life insurance is a miracle working tool. With the stroke of a pen and a small check you can create an instant estate or a trust fund to give a tax-free windfall to the people or organization that you care most about. Wow, who wouldn't want to do that? But when I talk to middle income families about their life insurance most of them only have the plan they get for free from work, or maybe a small plan they bought to cover their mortgage or their funeral costs. In most cases it does not amount to much and they usually don't really understand what it is they have or how it works.

I could probably write a whole book on the miracle of life insurance and the many different applications it can have in a well thought out financial plan but for now I just want to make sure you have your bases covered. If you have a spouse and/or children and they are dependent on your income then the most important use of life insurance for you may be to help you replace your income for your family in case you are not around to provide for them. If you love them, this is the least you would want for them. Especially if you could do so without breaking the bank, right? Let me give you a quick example. Let's say your annual income is $75,000 and you were to pass away last night. How much life insurance would you need to replace that $75,000 for your family? Let's assume that, whatever the amount of life insurance you buy, your spouse will invest that money safely in the bank or with a broker to earn a safe return of 5%. Take your income and divide your interest rate into it and you will find out how much death benefit you would need to properly replace your income for your family. ($75,000 / 5% = $1,500,000) Now you are probably thinking how expensive that would be but for a 40 year old male non-smoker in preferred health you are only talking about a premium of $66.35 per month on a 10 year term policy. Isn't your family's future worth $66.35? Now does this mean I am suggesting you go out and buy the largest term insurance plan you can afford and ignore the other important life insurance products such as Universal, Variable and Whole Life? No, not at all. I think all of these plans have important uses and it really just depends on what your objectives are. Most of my clients end up buying some term insurance and some permanent insurance as part of a carefully crafted financial plan that takes into account all of their needs and desires. As I said before life insurance can have many different applications in financial planning. But a great place to start is to make sure you are using it as it was intended, to take care of the ones you love and keep them in the world they are accustomed to in case you are not there to provide that world for them. What a beautiful gift to leave your family. They will never forget you. The best thing you can do is first, figure out how much you need. Then, get with a competent advisor who can help you structure that plan in the best way possible for you and your family.

Now that we've talked about many of the different types of insurance you can buy and how you can get yourself out of debt, our next section is going to talk about where to put all of the money you have been saving by getting out of debt and not overpaying for your insurance…

Chapter 6

Accessibility Is Important

Keep Your Money Where You Can Get It!

Have you ever had more month than you had money? Do you often suffer from the dreaded Italian disease, "MAFUNZSALOW"? (Translated My-Funds-Are-Low) But seriously, running out of money or coming up short is one of the most uncomfortable, stress producing events in your life. Who wants to lose sleep wondering if they will be able to make the bills this month? No one. Has this ever happened to you? Well, this section of the book can help you avoid this problem by teaching you how to hold on to more of your money. More importantly, you are about to discover some strategies and concepts that very few people have really thought about. Let's get started…

First of all, a while back in the section on paying off your debts, I talked about paying too much money to your credit cards and being so focused on paying off your debt that you never really accumulate any money. I feel like it is important to remind you again that if you are coming up short, maybe you are just trying to pay off your debts too quickly. Now I know that seems almost completely opposite of what any other financial writer has ever told you but when you think about it isn't it downright logical?

Let me give you an example to illustrate. Recently a longtime client of mine came in to review his financial plan with me. He like many others in our area has been hit hard by the slow economy in recent years. He was let go by his company and he thought that he would be back to work by now but he can't seem to find work anywhere. In fact things got so bad that he recently had to take a job in a convenience store making minimum wage to supplement his unemployment so that he can make the bills. As I started to review his situation, I asked him about his debts. Fortunately, he did not have many but he did have a $5,000 loan that he was paying $300 per month on. I asked him what his minimum payment was and he said about $113. I then asked him what his interest rate was on that money and he said he had recently rolled it over to a balance transfer offer that was offering him a 3.99% rate. So then I asked him, what to me was an obvious question, what is your hurry to pay off that debt? Here, he was in a dire situation wondering how he was going to make ends meet but instead of holding on to what little income he had so he could get by until he found a better circumstance, he was sending his credit card company almost $200 more than they were even asking for. Why?!? I will tell you why. It is because for years, he had been conditioned that debt is evil and must be eliminated at all costs no matter what. But is that always the case? Paying down debt quickly is not a bad idea in and of itself. But hurrying up to pay down your debts, when those debts may be keeping you from having the necessities, is just not practical. In fact, as we continued to talk, I found out that because of his recent job situation he was running around with no health insurance. For about the same amount of money he was using to pay his debt he was able to buy the much needed health insurance he was going without.

The point of this real life example is twofold. One: debt is not always evil and paying it down as fast as you can, may not be the best use of your money. Two: he may have never figured that out on his own because he had been trained by years of well-meaning people giving him bad advice to do otherwise. What I want you to get from this is have a plan to pay down your debt but don't use every spare nickel you have to do it and leave yourself short. After all, when the next emergency strikes and you used up all of your funds trying desperately to get out of debt where will you have to turn for help? That's right you will end up going right back into debt anyway. So, why not divert some (not all) of those debt paying dollars into emergency fund dollars?

Note: By the way, if you actually need cash to pay an unexpected bill (because they won't accept credit) what will happen when you use your credit card to get your extra cash back out? Won't they end up charging you an exorbitant interest rate just to use what could have been your own money?

Here is another strategy that flies in the face of conventional wisdom. Oh, and before I give it to you, what is so great about conventional wisdom anyway? Here is one of my all-time favorite quotes about conventional wisdom…

"That which has always been accepted by everyone, everywhere, is almost certain to be false." - Paul Valery (1871 – 1945)

So let's not worry about what the neighbors, your in-laws, or even what the self-proclaimed financial gurus think. Let's get serious and use our brains to make our own decisions. Anyway here is the second most popular cash flow crippler, paying extra money to your mortgage. Now, I know what you are thinking. How can that be a bad idea when almost everyone tells me that I should be paying that off as quickly as possible? And what about all of that interest? If I take the full 30 years to pay it off it will cost me almost 3 times what I paid for it. And how will I ever retire if I don't pay off my home?

Here is the biggest problem with that logic. It's just not safe! If you don't believe me think about this. Let's say you blindly follow the crowd and you put a large down payment on your home and pay an extra $100 or so to your mortgage every month to cut down on all of that evil interest you would have to pay otherwise. But then you find yourself in a position like the one I mentioned above where you are suddenly out of a job and don't have much in savings. Or maybe you didn't lose your job but you get sick and can't work, or you get into a bad car accident and are laid up in traction and won't be able to work for the next year or more. Now picture yourself walking into the bank and sitting at the little coffee table waiting for them to call your name.

You walk into your mortgage banker's office and you tell him your situation. Then you ask him or her with a humble smile. "You know all of that money I put down on my house? And you know all of those extra payments I have been sending you religiously because my brother in law the accountant told me it was such a good idea? I kind of need some of that money back. Can I just take that money back out of my home, just for a little while, just until I can get back on my feet?" What do you think that banker is going to say to you?

"I'd love to help you BUT…why don't you come back when you have some income?" You see your bank will only lend you money based on your ability to pay it back. It does not matter if that loan is backed up by bricks and mortar. They are not in the bricks and mortar business. They are in the cash flow business and if the cash isn't flowing they don't want your business. So, parking your money in your home is just not safe, especially if you don't have a large enough emergency fund. This is just another example of how most advice is geared to the already wealthy. Sure, if you are sitting on enough money in your savings account that you can weather any financial difficulty then maybe getting rid of that debt early is a good idea. But if you have no emergency funds, and no college plan for your kids, and no retirement plan, and not enough insurance to protect yourself and your family, then why on earth are you in a hurry to pay all of your money to a bank that is not about to help you when it all hits the fan? For most people putting extra money in your home is a very dangerous strategy.

Can you think of another place people park money that they can't get their hands on? How about their 401k plan or 403b or IRA or whatever they call your retirement plan at your job? Now, here we go again. I bet your conventional wisdom radar is all over this one. After all isn't your 401k the best savings and investment vehicle under the sun? That's what your human resource people said at that meeting at work. And I bet you even read an article in Money Magazine that said if you don't max out your retirement plan it's like throwing money out the window. But I remind you, who is most of that advice written for? That's right, the already wealthy. Are you already wealthy? If not, then please stop listening to them. Here is the problem. What happens if you max out your retirement plan at work and then life happens? How about, like in the mortgage example, you get sick, have an accident or lose your job, then what? Do you know what happens to your money in your retirement plan if you try and take it out before retirement? Full taxes plus a 10% penalty are due. Often times this can amount to 35% of your money or more gone as soon as you touch it. Ouch! Again, assuming you don't have a large enough emergency funds or a college fund for the kids, or enough money put away for retirement, or the right insurances in place, why are you tying your money up for the next 15 to 20 years in a place that you can't touch?

Note: many people are under the false assumption that due to a **hardship clause** you can get your money out if you really need it. **This is a fallacy!** IRA's do not have any hardship clause whatsoever, and some 401k type plans have it, but all it does is allow you access to your 401k money while you are not yet eligible. In other words they will let you have your own money **but full taxes and penalties still apply even if you have a hardship**.

As you can see, parking your money in the wrong place can be almost as bad as not saving it at all. Imagine the hardship of a family that losses their home with $50,000 or more of equity still trapped in it or the middle income worker who has spent his life accumulating $100,000 in a 401k only to be forced to pay $40,000 of that money to the government when he needed it most. Don't let this happen to you. Make sure you are putting your money where you can get it and that all of your immediate financial needs are being met long before you tie up your hard earned savings where you will not be able to get at it when you need it. Remember, deciding what financial areas need to be addressed first, and may get complicated so don't forget you can always get help from a financial professional skilled in this type of prioritizing of your cash flow.

But where do you put your money if paying down debt too quickly, paying off your mortgage too soon, and socking it all away in a retirement plan are not necessarily the best uses? How about if you instead sit down and create a true financial plan based on your most pressing needs and what's important to you? Are you most concerned about having enough money in an emergency fund, or is having the right amount of insurance in place to protect your family more important? The bottom line is, everyone has different priorities and sometimes by diverting the money you are tying up, you can start taking care of some of the other financial goals that might be more important to you. A good advisor can help you sort through all of these needs and may even be able to recommend financial products that help you use the same dollar to meet multiple needs. For example, there are financial products on the market right now where the money you put in can act as an emergency fund, an insurance benefit, and a retirement plan all at the same time. Do you think that might be a better use of the limited dollars you have to invest?

But let me ask you this unusual question…

Can Your Money Be Too Accessible?

I know I just spent a lot of time trying to prove to you by examples that unnecessarily tying your money up is almost always a bad idea, but what about the converse? Can you leave your money too liquid or accessible?

Before I answer that consider this. Have you ever started a savings plan? Do you have one now? How much do you have in it? How long have you been paying into it? Has it grown and grown over the years or does it grow to a certain point and then **end up spent?** Could it be that you don't really have a savings account at all? Maybe what you really have is a **"save-to-spend" account.**

Here is something that comes up quite often when I first meet with a client. I will ask if they are putting any money into savings and they will proudly tell me that they put $100 per month into a savings account. Then I ask them how long they have been doing that for and they tell me they have been saving like this for years.

Next I ask the big question, so how much is in that account now? The normal answer I get is almost always less than $1,000. Now tell me if this was a real savings account and not a "save-to-spend" account and you were putting $100 away for the last 5 years how much should you have in there? The correct answer is $6,000 plus interest gained. But why doesn't anybody seem to get that far? Could it be that their money was just too accessible?

By the way, having a "save-to-spend" account is a great idea. Particularly if you have a specific goal in mind and you use a separate savings account far away from the checking account you use to pay your bills. I started one this year to save for a family vacation to Disney. I went a few years ago on a credit card and it was a bitter sweet experience. I enjoyed the trip but in the back of my mind I knew that I was spending money I didn't have and that is never quite as satisfying. This year I plan to pay for the entire trip from savings and I already know I will enjoy it much more. And by the way, if I don't happen to save enough to go, I will just have to wait until I actually have the money. I know that may seem like a novel idea but our parents and grandparents lived that way all the time and most of them turned out pretty ok. (At least financially).

So, if you really want to have emergency money for a rainy day that you can fall back on, money that will make you feel a little more secure about your financial situation, then you need to set up a separate savings vehicle that is not as close as your local ATM. You need to park that money just far enough away that you will forget its even there and yet close enough that if you really do have an emergency (a 40% Off Sale at Macy's is not an emergency) you will be able to get your hands on the money in a reasonable amount of time. What investment or savings vehicle you use for this depends much on your personal situation so I won't go into detail here. But you may want to ask your advisor about something called an **Investment Grade Insurance Contract.** You can also Google that term. While these types of plans have many interesting benefits they are not right for everyone so as usual make sure you are working with someone who is taking into account your entire financial picture and not some product salesperson.

Now, let's look at another area of financial advice where Middle American workers have been taken advantage of on a grand scale…

Chapter 7

The Ups *Without* The Downs

Stop Losing Money. Period.

This is an area where you can clearly see that much of the advice being doled out today is really aimed at the wealthy. The problem is that too many Middle American investors are becoming casualties of this misdirected advice.

Maybe you have heard advice such as....

- *Over time investing in the stock market will yield the highest return possible.*

- *As long as you hold your investment for 10 years or more it is impossible to lose money long term.*

- *The real secret to investing is just "buy and hold". It is only the people who panic that lose out.*

- *If you want to make money in the market you have to diversify. If you spread your money among different asset classes you will reduce your risk.*

It all sounds so logical doesn't it? But has that been your personal experience? How much money have you really made in the stock market or in your mutual funds or in your 401k or IRA? If you look back over the last 10 years have you made money or would you have perhaps been better off in a safer alternative?

The problem is, the real answer for most Middle Americans is, they just don't know. They don't really pay much attention to their investments and so when you ask them if they are up or down they answer from their gut not from factual information. I know this because I ask this question of my clients and perspective clients every day and I get really lame answers. If I asked you, how has your 401k plan or your mutual fund portfolio done over the last 10 years what would you say? Could you tell me a specific rate of return that your account has earned? If you are like most of my clients you have not got a clue. In fact, what I find is that most people answer that question based on what % was written on their last statement. Does your last statement take into account all the ups and downs of the market over the last 10 years? No way. It basically just records where you are as of the statement date and what went on over the last 3 months. In fact, if you are adding to your account along the way, it is really hard to do the math to figure out if you are actually up or down. So most people just ignore it and they go with their gut. What else can they do?

Almost a year ago now I was working with one of my higher net worth clients. (No, not all of my clients are middle income, I will let one or two of the rich ones in now and then but they have to be fairly humble and believe me they are a rare breed.) This gentleman came in right before the market crash of 2008. And he was unhappy with his portfolio because he "felt like" it was going nowhere. He had over $200,000 in the brokerage account we were looking at and it was all invested in the market back in 1998 but he had no clue what his average rate of return was over those last 10 years. Why? Because he had other more important things in his life to attend to, I guess. The point is almost no one knows, so don't feel bad if you don't either. I gave him a fairly simple homework assignment. I told him to call the brokerage firm and find out what his cost basis was. (In English this means, how much did he invest in each fund?) He did as I asked and he came in to see me. Armed with this information we did some simple math and we found out that from 1998 to 2008 he had earned on average roughly about 1.5% per year. Was I surprised? No, not really. Because, I had done this for other clients before. He, on the other hand, was a little shocked. He knew he was not making as much as he would like but he had no idea he was making that little.

My point in sharing his example with you is twofold. First of all, most of us don't pay enough attention to have any business investing in the market. And secondly, most of us are making a lot less than we realize.

Now you might be thinking how can this be? After all, my boss or my brother in law makes all kinds of money in the market. Why can't I? First of all have you ever known anyone who liked to gamble? You know the uncle who played the ponies or the friend at work who buys $50 worth of lottery tickets every payday. You may even have a boss or a colleague who flies out to Vegas every couple of months to play their favorite game. Now, when was the last time you heard one of them bragging to you about how much money they lost? Have they ever told you about a really bad losing streak that was not followed with a story about how they made it all back? However, if you know anything about statistics you know that in the long run they will always lose because the odds are stacked against them. The point is when they do win; do they really sit down and think about how many times they had to lose to get to the win? What makes you think the stories about the big gains in the 401k or mutual funds are any different?

In fact let's take a quick look at some cold hard facts about investing in the market that your broker hopes you never find out about…

The first one I want to tell you about is a study that was done by a well-respected research firm known as Dalbar Inc. of Boston. They released a study in June of 2001 called,

"Quantitative Analysis of Investor Behavior." The study looked at actual investor returns from 1984 through the year 2000 compared to the S&P 500 market index.[6] (The S&P 500 is the leading benchmark used in the investment world. If you can beat the S&P 500 you are doing quite well) The S&P over that time frame averaged a whopping 16.3% average annual return. How do you think the average individual stacked up? Did they beat the S&P 500? Did they come close at least? No. The average equity mutual fund investor only made 5.32% and that was during one of the best bull markets in history.

I hope this is beginning to put this in perspective for you. If you have been promised by some mutual fund sales person or stock broker that you will average 8%, 10% or even 12% returns in the market you may be in for a rude awakening.

By the way Dalbar Inc. published similar studies in 1994 and 1998 and found similarly stunning results. But they are not the only ones to study how well or poorly the average individual investor performs in the market. Here is another study…

This one was conducted in June of 2002 by Charles Trzcinka professor of finance at Indiana University. The study was published in *Money* magazine. His study ran from 1998 through 2001 and analyzed 6,900 U.S. stock mutual funds. Professor Trzcinka concluded that while the average mutual fund over that period gained 5.7% the average investor earned only a paltry 1% gain. The large difference between the funds stated returns and the amount investors actually realized was a surprise even to Professor Trzcinka.

---

[6] Indices are unmanaged and investors cannot invest directly in an index. Unless otherwise noted, performance of indices do not account for any fees, commissions or other expenses that would be incurred. Returns do not include reinvested dividends.

The Standard & Poor's 500 (S&P 500) is an unmanaged group of securities considered to be representative of the stock market in general. It is a market value weighted index with each stock's weight in the index proportionate to its market value.

Now, you might be saying to yourself sure those numbers are bad because you are only looking at average individual investors. I know that investing is not my game so I seek out trained professionals who manage my mutual fund for me and I only select fund managers with excellent track records. Or you may be someone who subscribes to one of those very chic investment newsletters and the investment genius who runs your newsletter can prove beyond the shadow of a doubt that his strategies have outperformed the market time and time again. Well, I hate to burst your bubble but the professionals seem to do just as poorly as the average guy when it comes to picking and managing a portfolio. Just look at the data.

The vast majority of mutual fund managers have performed far worse than the indexes investors are paying them to beat. According to a recent study done by Lipper Analytical Services, 94% of all mutual funds under perform the indexes they are trying to beat. You may have heard of Morningstar. They are famous for rating mutual funds. However, their research showed that during the 10 year period that ended in 1998 the Wilshire 5000[7] index outperformed a collection of highly performing mutual funds that they selected by an average of 7.2%. (The Wilshire 5000 is another benchmark that is much broader than the S&P 500 as it is based on a conglomerate of many more companies. It has been likened to buying the entire stock market as it contains most U.S. stocks instead of just 500 companies like the S&P 500)

And if you still don't believe me, all you have to do is buy a copy of *Money* magazine. Look at the top 10 mutual funds then look at them again next year. You will notice that you will more than likely see 10 entirely different funds. In fact, if you do some digging you more than likely will find that the top 10 funds from last year are now performing at the bottom of the list. Without consistency, a flash in the pan

[7] The Wilshire 5000 Total Market Index, or more simply the Wilshire 5000, is a market-capitalization-weighted index of the market value of all stocks actively traded in the United States.

performance can only be attributed to nothing more than luck.

Now, let's not forget about the investment gurus that produce investment newsletters. Often, they dazzle us with their layers of complexity, claiming to have the secret formula as it were on how to pick stocks or the best funds. However, Hulbert Financial Digest did a study between August 1987 and December 1998 and they found that the average fund newsletter's model portfolio provided a return of only one half of the Wilshire 5000 index. The Wilshire 5000 averaged 14.1% and the average newsletter portfolio averaged only 7.3% during that same time frame. They were beat by a landslide. Only 6 out of 55 advisors did better than the market, yet all of them claimed that their complex strategies would implicitly provide market beating returns.

With these miserable statistics does it make any sense for Middle American investors to continue to gamble their money away? Does the end justify the means? Is it worth it to put 100% of your own money at risk to earn often times less than you could have using much safer alternatives? Or worse yet, what if the market tanks just when you need your money most? Can you as a Middle American worker and investor afford to take what little money you have been able to squirrel away and risk it in the stock market?

But if investing in the market is not the place to put your money then where should it go?

Market Linked Strategies

What if you had the ability to earn unlimited amounts based on increases in the indexes we have been talking about but with no risk to your principal ever? What if all of your money could be guaranteed safe regardless of stock market performance? This Strategy gives you a unique opportunity to participate in the upside with no downside. Have you ever heard the saying have your cake and eat it too?

Picture your friends complaining about losses in the market. You quietly say nothing, knowing that your money is actually growing while they see month after month, their brokerage statements showing a declining value.

Here is how it works…

1) Your principal is 100% guaranteed no matter what happens to the market.

2) If the index you select is up you receive the entire gain minus a predetermined spread.

3) If the index you select is down you keep all of your money and start over.

Depending on the actual product you usually get to select from multiple indexes like the S&P 500, the Dow Jones, the Euro Stock 50[8] and so on. In some products you can even link your return to the price of gold which happens to be a very trendy investment as I write this book due to a very shaky global economy and a weak dollar.

Let's look at one quick example that I show many of my clients who are fed up with the stock market and are looking for safer alternatives where they can still earn a better than average return compared to most bank products.

Let's say you start with $100,000 and your money is directly invested in the stock market. Now let's say that by the end of year one the market has dropped by 10%, how much do you

---

[8] The Dow Jones Industrial Average (DJIA) is a price-weighted average of 30 actively traded "blue chip" stocks, primarily industrials, but includes financials and other service-oriented companies. The components, which change from time to time, represent between 15% and 20% of the market value of NYSE stocks.

The Dow Jones Euro Stoxx 50 is a market capitalization-weighted stock index of 50 large, blue-chip European companies operating within Eurozone nations. The universe for selection is found within the 18 Dow Jones EURO STOXX Super sector indexes, from which members are ranked by size and placed on a selection list.

have left in your investment? That's right $90,000. ($100,000 - $10,000 loss = $90,000)

Now let's say year two comes along and the market is up 10% how much do you have at the end of year two? Well if you said $100,000 you are a little off and here is why. This is a bit of a trick question. $90,000 times10% = $9,000. Add that $9,000 to the $90,000 you had left at the end of year one and how much do you have now? If you said $99,000 then you are with me.

The point is that the market went down by 10% and then up by 10% and you ended up with a loss. It doesn't seem fair but that is the math and it proves that your money has to work even harder to come back from a loss and those stock market losses can be very detrimental to you over time.

Now, is it safe to say that from time to time the market will actually go backwards and so if you invest directly in the market you are likely to lose money at least now and again?

What if we could take all of those down years out of the equation, how much better off would you be? That is how this market linked strategies work. Let's take a look at this same example, only this time we were smart enough to invest in a market linked strategy instead of directly plunking our money into the market and risking everything.

Now let's say you are starting with $100,000 only this time you are in a safe guaranteed market linked strategy. Let's say the market takes the same 10% loss. How much do you have? If you said $100,000 you are right! Remember your principal is contractually guaranteed. You cannot lose money.

Now year two comes along and the market is up 10% do you think this strategy will pay you the full 10%? No, that would be too good to be true. Let's say the strategy you picked along with your advisors help had a 3% spread. That means in English (not investment jargon) that the company who set up the contract gets to keep 3% (but only when you win). So if the market were up 10% the company keeps 3% and you keep 7%. And 7% of $100,000 is $7,000 so now you have $107,000 at the end of year two. Not too shabby.

Now which investor would you rather be? The guy in the first scenario that had 100% of his money at risk directly invested in the market and ended up after two years with $99,000 or the guy who never lost a moments sleep knowing his money was always safe and ended up with $107,000?

Do you know what my clients almost always say when I explain this strategy to them?
"Why doesn't everyone do this?" And do you know what I tell them? Everyone is doing this. *You* just have not heard about it yet. And that is the truth. It has been my experience that once people fully understand these opportunities they generally move their money as soon as possible.

Now, so far all I have explained is the strategy not the products that make this strategy available. There are actually several formats that you can select from when purchasing products that use the Market Linked Strategies. I don't want to get into specific product with you for two reasons. First, which product you use depends on a multitude of factors, like how old you are, what tax bracket you are in, how long of a time frame before you will need the money, where the money is coming from and so on. So, in giving you a general view of the available products, I would most likely be doing you a disservice. Two, the products that use these strategies are some of the most misunderstood and misrepresented products on the market and I fear that a casual mention of the product (without a lengthy and complicated explanation) would send you down a road of misconstrued ideas and half-truths. Also, my desire in writing this book is to share with you the principals that have helped me and my clients be more financially secure, not to sell you on one particular product or strategy.

Ultimately, if you decide to go this route you will have to buy these products from someone who has a license to sell them. The problem is there are a lot of sales hacks who really don't know what they are talking about and then there are a few seasoned professionals who can guide you with this process. The good news is if you live in the Rockford Metro area you can always ask me for help. (I happened to be licensed in these areas.) And the better news is, if you don't, I will be giving you some guidance on how you can find a qualified advisor who has specialized training not only in these strategies but in many of the other concepts I have been sharing with you. (Hint, we all have the same mentor so we tend to think alike) But more on that later. Now let's talk about our next important principal of financial security…

Chapter 8

How To Avoid Paying More Taxes Than You Should[9]

Stop Giving Your Money To The Government.

I heard it said once that tax avoidance is a civil liberty while tax-evasion will get you 10 to 20. So, most of us want to stay out of the realm of tax evasion but who wants to pay more than their fair share of taxes? Now, as a Middle American worker and investor you might think that you don't make enough money to have to worry that much about taxes but in reality nothing could be further from the truth. Often times it is the Middle American worker that gets hit the hardest. Think about it, the poor don't pay taxes. In fact, as it stands right now the top 50% of all wage earners pay about 97% of all income taxes. While this may not seem fair the truth is the government feels sorry for poor people and figure they have a hard enough time as it is just getting by. Now the top 20% or so are usually business owners and as a business owner what do you have that most middle income Americans don't have? Write off's. Business owners get to buy all sorts of stuff that they would probably buy anyway and they buy it with pre-tax dollars because they can claim the business needed it. Now, this may be a bit of an overstatement and of course the IRS has their guidelines but many purchases are at least partially deductible for the business owner. So, who

[9] Pursuant to requirements imposed by the Internal Revenue Service, any tax advice contained in this communication (including any attachments) is not intended to be used, and cannot be used, for purposes of avoiding penalties imposed under the United States Internal Revenue Code or promoting, marketing or recommending to another person any tax-related matter. Please contact us if you wish to have formal written advice on this matter

gets stuck paying all of the taxes? In many cases the Middle American worker. But what can you do about it? You can be smart about your money. You can and should learn that it really is not so important sometimes how much you make, because it all comes down to how much do you get to keep?

Here is another reason you should be concerned about taxes. Believe it or not, at the time of the writing of this book taxes are on sale. We are living in one of the best tax environments this country has ever seen. I know it may not feel like it when you look at how much the government is taking out of your check each pay period. But, if you look at the top tax brackets from 1914 to today the average top bracket is 61.5% with the worst taxes being charged in the 1950's and 1960's when the top bracket was a whopping 91%. Today the top tax bracket is only 35%; so as I said, taxes are on sale. But what happens to all sales? They are usually for a limited time only, right? What do you think may happen to our tax rates going forward? If you are not sure, just look at the facts.

Government programs like Social Security and Medicare are in trouble, and where is the government going to get the money to bail them out? The war this country has been fighting was financed on credit, where are they going to get the money? Millions of Baby Boomers are all going to retire at the same time putting even more strain on the social programs, where are they going to get the money? People are living much longer than was ever expected putting more and more strain on Social Security and Medicare, the government bailed out the banking system with money they are printing as I write this, the economic stimulus checks were paid for with borrowed money. Where will all of this money come from? Are taxes going to be higher in the future? You can pretty much bank on it.

So what can we do about it? Again we need to be diligent and start taking an interest in how much of our money is going to the government and look for legal, ethical ways to reduce these burdens. I will attempt to point out a few of these strategies in this section of the book. I can't cover every situation so my advice to you is partner with a competent tax advisor who can help you avoid paying more than your fair share of taxes. But here are some things you can do right away to cut down on how much money you have to share with your Uncle Sam.

Do you own a home based business? If you do then you are already on the right track with this one as this can help you add some tremendous tax savings. If you don't own one why not consider starting one at least part time? Besides the tax-breaks you can actually earn some extra money on the side. Now, you might be thinking that you are no business person and you work hard enough at your nine to five jobs. But this does not have to be a big undertaking. Even something as simple as joining an MLM (Multi-Level Marketing) company and running it from your home counts and can lead to some significant tax breaks.

Now, I feel a brief word of caution here is appropriate. While I like the idea of starting an MLM or Network Marketing business for the home based business tax breaks make sure it is something that you will actually enjoy and follow through with. Also, be careful not to get caught up in the hype. While I have found some terrific opportunities in these companies even the ones I like tend to oversell the dream and people get all caught up in it thinking this will be the answer to all of their economic problems. The problem is that it seldom works out as easy as they say it will. So if it sounds too good to be true it probably is. But this does not mean you should write the whole idea off (no pun intended). My wife and I personally run at least two MLM businesses currently and they are both companies I would highly recommend. My wife sells Jafra cosmetics and usually makes enough money from her small client base to pay for all of her makeup and spa products and sometimes she actually has money left over. It took her several years to build but all she did is stay in touch with the people who bought and she developed repeat customers. I also like this company because they have very high profit margins even for beginners and it is a product that needs to be replenished so your clients have to keep coming back to you.

The other company I like and I promote is Pre-Paid Legal. I have not made enough money to quit my day job yet but it does provide me with some extra income. Also, I promote it mainly because I think their service is amazing. It is almost like having an Attorney on retainer without the hefty price tag. I promote it because I believe in it and I make some money sharing this idea with my friends and clients. For me it is a win-win.

Another way you can start a home based business is to find something you like to do like a hobby or a craft and turn that into a business. My wife is into crafts and I am into starting businesses. So for one of our anniversaries I bought her a video training series that showed you how to take gold and silver wire to wrap gemstones. It was a lot of fun and I even made a few pieces of jewelry myself. We then would go to high end art fairs and sell her wares. On more than one occasion we made $700 just sitting around for a weekend art fair and we had fun doing it. We stopped doing it for now because we have two toddlers running around and that pretty much keeps her busy.

The bottom line is starting a home based business can be an enjoyable endeavor and you can save big money on your taxes in the meantime. If you have an office or a workshop in your home you can deduct a proportionate percentage of the home bills you already pay. Imagine getting a tax break just for paying your own electric, heating, phone, or internet bill that you were going to pay anyway. The tax code favors business owners so if you are inclined to do so think about becoming one. You may just thank me for it.

Now let's talk about saving taxes on your savings and investments. If all you have is a "save to spend account" taxes have probably not been much of an issue for you. The problem there is like we talked about earlier you are not letting your money grow long enough for it to start earning any real compound interest. But now you know better. You know that putting extra money to your debt, and to your home, and to unnecessary insurance plans, and even to your 401k plan may be preventing you from accumulating any real emergency money or available savings. Now let's say that we have gone over all of that and we found some money for you to invest. Then by redirecting some of that money that was previously not working for you as hard as it could have you were able to find $500 per month or more.

Note: While this may sound like a lot of money it is actually quite common for financial advisors trained in the found money strategies to help their clients come up with of monthly savings without asking them to give up or make changes to their current lifestyle. I will show you how to find an advisor trained in these methods in the section marked **Get Better Advice.**

What would you do with it? If you put that money into a fully taxable account eventually you would have some real tax problems. By the way, a fully taxable account is a savings account, money market or mutual fund that has no tax shelter. These are quite common and what most people use for their "save to spend" accounts. There are a few people that get really good at saving all on their own. You know those self-disciplined type people. And often this is a mistake they make. They are good at saving money but no one has ever showed them where to put it.

So what kind of tax problems do you have in a fully taxable account? Well, first of all every time you earn interest you are basically taking 3 steps forward and one step back. For example, perhaps your account is a money market account that pays 5% interest and you are in a 28% tax bracket. What is 28% of 5%? If you said 1.4% you would be right. So you earn 5% then at the end of the year you have to report that interest to the government and they take 1.4% of it leaving you with a paltry 3.6% after taxes. Wouldn't you rather keep the entire 5%? Of course you would! But before I show you how to do that, let's look at one more reason why this is such a big problem.

After all you might be thinking that you won't feel that tax very much because it only comes out at tax time and you will just get a little smaller tax return, so even though you are paying it you really don't feel it that much. This is true in the beginning but what about latter on.

If you saved $500 per month and earned 5% interest on it in 20 years you would have $206,373 if you paid all of the taxes out of your income each year. But the problem is that will get harder and harder to do. Why? When you have $206,373 saved your interest that year will be $10,318 and the tax due at the end of the year will be $2,889. That is a lot of money to have to come up with at tax time even if you are used to getting a tax return. In fact, if you were to save up for that big end of the year tax bite you would need to save $240 per month just to pay the taxes. That's nearly half the $500 per month you have been investing. You put in $500 and the government wants $240 back. Isn't that like taking one step forward to take one step back? Unfortunately our tax code punishes savers unless they learn to make some smarter moves with their money. You need to learn some smarter moves.

So what do we do instead? Some people like to put their money into tax-deferred savings or investment vehicles because then they can earn interest on their interest without having to pay Uncle Sam at the end of the year. If you want to defer taxes you can use an annuity, or an IRA, 401k, 403b and so forth. If you use a government regulated plan not only are your taxes on your earnings deferred but you can even lower your taxes on your income because you get to write off the amount you place into these accounts up to certain limits.

You get a front end tax break as if you never even earned that money allowing you to pay less income tax and then the money gets to sit in there and grow year after year without having to report any of that growth on your tax return. Now I know what you are thinking, this sounds like the greatest thing going how do I get more of these government regulated tax-deferred accounts? But hold on. Remember, we already talked about one of the problems with these accounts is that there are a lot of strings attached if you should need your money early. And this may not be a good idea if you have not solved all of your other more pressing financial issues like having an emergency fund and the proper insurances and a savings for the kids' college or whatever goals you might have. But actually there is another even bigger problem with these accounts that we have not begun to talk about…

What Happens When You Finally Retire And Want To Get Your Money Out?

You would think that if you let the government keep your money hostage according to plan rules until you reach age 59½ that when you finally get there you could take it out free and clear but that is not the case! The good news is you will be past the point of a so called "early withdrawal" so you won't be charged a penalty but remember none of that money had ever been taxed. Do you think the government is going to let you take it out and spend it without taking their fair (or unfair) share?

They can't wait to tax you on that money and if income taxes will be higher by the time you retire (like most people who have paid any attention to government spending recently have determined) then you will pay dearly every time you tap that account.

But rest assured says the government (who want desperately for you to fund your own retirement since social security is in such turmoil) and your plan administrator (who is associated with a mutual fund company who desperately wants you to buy their funds)...

"You will be in a lower tax bracket when you retire than when employed".

While this may have been true at one time and for people in certain income brackets, today for many of us this is a big MYTH!

With the 1986 Tax Reform Act and subsequent tax reform, most retirees in America will find themselves in a tax bracket at least as high—if not higher—than during their earning years. Why?

Prior to 1986 when people retired they were entitled to double exemptions. This retirement tax break *no longer exists*. In addition to this most of the deductions that were helping them all those years are now gone. Think about it. They have a free and clear home so they no longer have the mortgage interest expense deduction. Not to mention their children have matured into adults so they can no longer claim them. If they were running a business they are now retired so they lost all of their business exemptions. With all of your tax deductions gone do you really think you will be in a much lower tax bracket?

In fact, *US News and World Report* published an article in 1989 by Leo Weidner entitled, "How Congress Is Peddling IRA and 401(k) Snake Oil." Mr. Weidner had this to say, "One of the original IRA and 401(k) tenets held that deferring tax until retirement was advantageous because funds would likely be taxed at a lower rate. That is no longer axiomatic. You may well spend retirement in the same or higher bracket if you accumulate a respectable retirement nest egg. In fact, tax rates will likely rise in the future to cover budget deficits."

Let's take a look at a quick example of how taxes can rob a good portion of your income in retirement....

Why Your 401(k), Or IRA, May Be A Ticking Tax Time Bomb!

Let's take a look at an example...

If a married couple age 35 contributed $4,000 per year into a 401(k) or IRA between now and their age 65, they would have contributed $120,000 over that 30 year period.

Now let's assume that this couple was in the 27% Federal tax bracket and let's assume that the State tax rate is 7%. So their total combined tax rate is 34% per year.

So if their $4,000 per year contribution is tax-deductible (and it is) they would be saving 34% of that contribution off their income taxes for that year.

34% of $4,000 is $1,360 of tax savings each year. So over a 30 year period they saved $40,800. (30 Years X $1,360 = $40,800)

Most people STOP here and say hey that's great look at how much money they saved. **But this is only half of the story...**

Let's keep looking and see what really happens to that $40,800 savings once they retire. To keep the numbers simple let's say that their account grew **tax –deferred** at an average rate of 10% per year for the 30 years. They would have $723,774 in their account. ($4,000 per year X 30 years at 10% growth per year = $723,774)

Note: I don't think it is realistic to assume that your money will actually grow at a 10% rate but it is ironic that the same gurus who tell you that you can easily earn 10% in the stock market are also the people who encourage you to max out your 401k plan. So I use this example this way with these numbers to "kill them with their own poison" so to speak. Let's look at why their advice just does not work out.

Now let's say they retire and they continue to make an average return of 10% per year and then withdraw that interest to live on in retirement. See the table below…

Age 65 401(k) or IRA Balance	$723,774
	X 10%
Annual Withdrawal at Retirement	$72,377
Tax Bracket	X 34%
Annual Tax	($24,608)
Net Income in Retirement after Taxes	=$47,769

Look at the amount of annual tax they will actually pay ($24,608). You will notice that in the first two years of retirement they will pay back *more* money to the government than they saved during their 30 years of contributing! ($24,608 X 2 = $49,216 – *total savings of* $40,800 = **$8,416** ***MORE TAX then they saved!)***

What's worse is a person living a normal life expectancy will pay back well over **10 times** what they actually saved in their earning years.

So, while *tax-deferral* is better than the pay as you go *fully taxable* accounts we already talked about the tax savings is really just not there in the long run for many Middle American savers. If fully taxable is no good and tax-deferred is not much better then what can you do?

How About A Tax-Free Account

Does that really exist you might ask? Yes. In fact, it not only exists it comes in assorted colors and flavors. You just have to know how to set one up properly and what the right one is for you.

So what is a tax-free account and how do they work? The basic premises is that you put your money in and earn interest on your interest every year just like in the tax-deferred account only here, if you follow the rules you can actually pull your money out income tax free when you need it. One example of such an account is the government regulated Roth IRA or the new Roth 401k option. I think both of these plans are a great move in the right direction. However, they still have many government rules and restrictions and so I prefer to put my money in non-regulated tax-free accounts. But does all of this talk of tax-free money sound almost too good to be true? Are you wondering…?

What's the catch?

Well, here is the catch but I think it is really more of a trade off than a catch. When you set up a tax-free account you don't get to write off any of the money you contribute. This means all of your contributions go in after you already paid tax on them. Does this make these plans a bad idea because you are missing out on some great tax-deduction?

Ask yourself this question. Would I rather pay tax on a small amount of money now or pay tax on a large amount of money latter? You would probably pick paying tax on the smaller amount of money now to get it out of the way before it gets worse, right? Or how about this, would I rather pay tax now while I am working and can afford it or later when I am too old or sick to work and will be trying to live off of my savings? You would probably rather pay the tax now wouldn't you. In fact when has it ever been a good idea to put off paying something now that you can truly afford to pay only to pay it later when the burden has mushroomed?

Earlier I mentioned a product called an Investment Grade Insurance Contract. This product is one of the only ones I know of that allows you fairly liberal access to your own money if you should need it, and protects you from stock market losses by offering you strong guarantees, and it also lets you get your money out without paying income tax. However, this product is not right for everyone and some clients might be better off with a Roth IRA or Roth 401 depending on their situation. The Investment Grade Insurance Contracts biggest flaw is that it is often misunderstood by most financial advisors. In fact, most of the people who are licensed to sell this product don't fully understand it's potential. Personally, I have been involved with marketing these products for the last 16 years and for my first 10 years of helping people with them I am ashamed to say that I did not fully understand the value of what I was recommending and often underutilized this important financial tool. But again, to try and explain any product in a few paragraphs in a book like this would not do it justice so the best thing I can tell you is if you want to learn more read the section on how to find an advisor who is not only licensed but who really knows what he/she is talking about.

To sum this topic up remember that taxes are important and will impact you in a major way to your detriment if you don't pay close attention to them. Also, look for ways not only to defer your taxes but to avoid them all together when possible. Now let's talk about a principal so simple yet so powerful that it can mean the difference between financial failure and success…

Chapter 9

The Secret To Saving More Money

Pay Yourself First!

Have you ever heard that expression before? You probably have as I am definitely not the first financial advisor to heed this mantra. But what does it mean and how do you do it? To get the answers to these questions we need to dig a little deeper.

Ask yourself this question. Is there ever a good time to put money away? Or how about this, how much extra money do you have at the end of the month after all of the bills are paid? The correct answers are No and None. But why? Why do some people seem to be so good at saving and others are just horrible? Why can some people who make only a modest income manage to save large amounts of money each month while other people with 6 figure incomes spend more than they make every year? The answer is it has everything to do with your attitude or as one author I know called it your moneytude. How much money you are able to save often has more to do with how important saving is to you verses how much so called "expendable" income you have.

In my dealing with people just this year I met a couple who make a high six figure income and they managed to make it all the way to their mid-40's and had not saved a dime. I also met a woman who only made about $34,000 per year and she managed to save $500 per month and she had been on some incredible vacations and didn't owe anything to anyone except her small student loans.

Now, I know our economy is in a shambles and many people are losing their jobs and the overtime that was once there is no longer available. But, these should not be excuses not to save. These should be motivators too save. How long would your savings last if you did lose your job? What if unemployment runs out and you still have not found work? Shouldn't you be saving while you still have income to save?

I know it is not easy and I have heard all of the excuses. But ask yourself, in the last week did you spend $20 that you didn't absolutely have to spend? How about the week before that? And the week before that? Is what you spent that money on really more important than your financial security? Now I am not talking to those of you who may be in crisis mode and just trying not to foreclose on your home because you lost your job. But if that is not you, what really keeps you from putting more money away?

There is an irrefutable law of money and once you understand it you can use this deeper knowledge to breakthrough your reluctance to save. Here it is…

Expenses Always Rise To Meet Income. Always!

Have you ever gotten a raise and thought how much easier your life will be because of it only to find out that within a few months you were having just as much trouble keeping up with your bills as you had before the raise? Have you ever cut your expenses figuring that by getting rid of cable and not eating out you were going to save a whole lot of money? What happened? After a few months you seemed like you were right back where you started only now you didn't have cable anymore. Your thinking seemed correct but you were forgetting about the irrefutable law of money. This law is so true because it really has nothing to do with money and everything to do with human nature. We all want more. And the more we get the more we want. It really is not easy to live simply. It is an admirable goal and we probably all could stand to work on it a little more but when it comes down to it no matter how much we cut back or how much we earn it never is enough is it? There is always something right around the corner to spend that money on. Just think about your wish list. I know you have one, we all do.

Is it wrong or somehow financially irresponsible to have a wish list? I don't think so, as long as you realize that you may not get all of it accomplished in the next month or so. The bottom line is we all have things we need and things we just want, but we can't have it all and we certainly can't have it all this week, no matter what that guy at the home loan center at your bank tells you.

The point is you will never have ENOUGH money and if you wait until all your bills are paid or all of your wants or even needs are met before you start saving you will NEVER have any money. Is that what you want?

How would you feel if you could have $25,000 or $50,000 or even $200,000 saved for emergencies, your future or whatever comes up? How would you feel if you were able to save that money in an accessible tax advantaged account where you could in effect create your own bank? How about if the next time you needed money for a major purchase you didn't have to go ask the bank for a loan like you were asking your Mommy for allowance? What if, instead, you could go to your own private bank and borrow your own money out and pay yourself back so you would have the money again when your next wish list item was ready to be financed?

Note: By the way if you want to learn more about the be your own bank idea you can visit my website https://financialsecurity.video/6058/51 for a free video that explains this concept better than I could do it justice in this book. It will ask you for your email but it only goes to me and I will not share it with anyone.

The good news is it is really pretty simple to start paying yourself first. All you have to do is decide that it is important to you. You have to realize that a percentage of everything you make is yours to keep. You worked hard for it and if you don't put some of that away you really have no one to blame but you. Stop looking for reasons why you can't and like the sneaker people say, just do it.

Exercise: Try this. If you really don't think you are able to save anything and you just don't see how you can than start small. For the next 3 months I want you to take your paycheck and as soon as you cash it multiply your paycheck by 1%. Or if you don't know how to use your % key on your calculator multiply it by .01. So if you made $650 you would multiply that by .01 and that would equal $6.50. Take that $6.50 and open a savings account. Repeat this with every paycheck for at least 3 months then raise that % to .03 for the next 3 months. See if you can raise it up every 3 months, and you will be surprised about how much money you can save if you just take it off the top instead of trying to save what is left over.

Found Money

What is found money and where can you get some? Good question! Well we already talked about a few places right here in this book. We talked about putting too much towards your debt without developing the habit of saving. We talked about some of the problems with putting too much money toward your mortgage and why that is not safe. We talked about tying your money up for 15, 20 , or even 30 years in a government regulated retirement plan before you have all of your short term needs taken care of.

We even talked about buying the loser insurance plans that suck money out of your pocketbook that could easily be put to better use. Or how about the money you are paying to the government when you pay more in taxes than you could have. These are all areas that I call found money. But how do you know you found as much of it as you could and what do you do with it when you find it?

If you read this book and you realize that you have some money in your budget that you might be able to reallocate for a better use and then you just add that back to your budget what do you think will happen to all of that money? That's right. **Expenses Always Rise To Meet Income. Always.** You remembered the rule. So before long, you will go back to feeling broke at the end of the month and you will have nothing to show for it. Here is my suggestion.

Why not get with an advisor who has been trained in these found money strategies and make sure you found all of yours. Then let that advisor find out what is really important to you. What are your most important priorities and goals, your dreams, the things you want to see happen in your life? Is the most important thing to you making sure that your children will be able to have a college education? Did you have a parent that never saved any money and ended up working long beyond when they would have liked to and you want to make sure that doesn't happen to you? Or do you just want to get a handle on things by getting your bad debts paid off and having enough money in the bank that you can handle a financial crisis without panicking? Maybe you aren't sure what is really important to you yet and you need a little help sorting out your priorities. A good financial advisor will talk with you and listen to you and draw you out until you both know what your most important goals are. Then that same advisor will help you find the money to get started working on those goals and suggest some financial products to go along with that plan and help you on your way. The point is, don't just find the money and blow it, find the money and use it to fund your plan. But in order to fund your plan you need to get serious about creating one.

So how do you find an advisor that can help you do all of this.

Chapter 10

How To Finally Get The Right Advice

Seek Out Better Advice

I called this section **Seek Out Better Advice** because I am assuming that the advice you are getting now is substandard. I make that assumption because if middle income Americans were getting great advice most of us would not be in such dire financial shape. I also know for a fact that most people are getting sub-standard advice because I don't just sit in my office writing books, I actually run a financial consulting business where I meet with several new families every single week, and the truth is in most cases they really aren't getting any advice at all. For the most part they are being sold a hodge-podge of financial products by financial salesman to meet one need at a time and no one is really sitting down with them to create a plan.

I also know this to be true because no one has ever walked into my office and said, "Here is my current plan how can you improve upon it?" The facts are no one really has a plan. They own products, they were sold products, but they don't have a plan. So my advice is to simply get some real advice and stop listening to the product pitchmen. Your plan needs to go beyond the products and actually solve your financial problems.

When you finally meet with an advisor that is the real deal you will know it by how your first conversation goes. If he/she asks you a lot of questions and tries to really understand what your concerns are there is a good chance you have found the right person. They should be spending most of their time in that first meeting trying to fully understand what it is that you want and how they can best help you. Your gut feeling should be telling you that this person has your best interest at heart and is not just trying to push a product on you. If you are not getting that feeling then look elsewhere. If you were about to have heart surgery, would you go with the first guy you talk to or would you stay with a doctor you had been going to for years out of loyalty? Or would you talk to the two or three best doctors in the area ask them your questions and go with your gut? I think you know the answer. Why should choosing your financial advisor be any different? This could mean the difference between being financially secure or being a complete financial mess.

Throughout this book I told you that I would help you to find competent advice and now I am going to make good on that promise. First of all, I would hope that after reading this book if you live in the Rockford Metro area and I am still alive and kicking (after all this book may just be around longer than me, but I am only 40 so I should be here for a long time) that you would at least call me as one of the advisors you consider. But many people reading this book will want someone close to home; so here are some more tips on how you can find someone who is likely to be trained in at least some of the strategies that I have been talking with you about.

How to find a competent financial professional?

I believe in giving credit where credit is due and many of the ideas that I teach I would never have learned if I had not met a man named Lew Nason. Lew has developed some incredible training for financial professionals and I have personally been trained by him and have talked with many of the people he has trained. I am telling you this because Lew has a great website where you can locate advisors in your area that have taken his courses. This won't insure you have the right person but most of the advisors who take Lew's class focus on working with Middle American families and understand your concerns. You can visit this website at www.foundmoneyconsultants.com.

Another thing that you can check out when looking for a competent financial professional, are their designations. Now last time I checked there were at least 89 different designations doled out by about 87 different financial services associations and professional institutions.

An advisor might be a CAC, CEP, CFA, CFP, CLU, CHFC, RFA, RIA, CSA, AEP, FIC, LUTCF, and there are even the ones I have RFC & FMM. But with all of this alphabet soup how do you know what it all means, and can it really help you in determining if your advisor is qualified to help you?

Obviously, we don't have room in this book to go into all 89 designations and break them down for you, and you probably have more important things to do with the rest of your day than to read about the various financial planning designations. However, the professional institutions that create and monitor these designations do provide a valuable service. Currently there are no consistent licensing requirements for the various persons who call themselves "financial advisors" so the public has a critical need for a method of distinguishing the qualified and dedicated financial advisor from the know it all down the block who woke up one day and decided to hang out a shingle. Organizations like the IARFC (International Association of Registered Financial Consultants) and others require their members not only to adhere to a strict code of ethics but also they must meet other requirements to become and stay an active member. For example, the IARFC requires all of its members to meet and document 7 separate stringent requirements in the areas of education, experience, examinations, integrity, licensing, ethics and significant continuing professional education. But even if your advisor has earned one of these coveted designations does that really make him/her trustworthy? After all he/she may have met all of the requirements and still be dishonest. In fact, there are still many loopholes in today's regulatory systems and even seemingly ethical advisors with credentials may have a past record of doing the wrong thing and it may be harder than you think to find out about it.

Some of the problems with the current system include, regulatory agencies allowing both investment and insurance advisors to do business even after they've been convicted of a serious violation against public interest. Investment "professionals" can be convicted of perpetrating an investment scam in one state, then move to another state to commit the same crime. What about how about the problem of an advisor being barred from the securities business only to later open an insurance business? How about the fact that sometimes one regulatory agency such as the SEC may not have the same information about an individual that another regulatory agency like FINRA might have?

Once again we are left in a quandary, with so many regulatory loopholes how do we know who we can trust? Wouldn't it be great if you could just do an affordable background check on any advisor you are even thinking of doing business with and it would cover all of the areas mentioned above and more? Well, now you can! Recently two organizations known as the National Ethics Bureau and another company known as Advisor Check have made this service available to the general public.

The answer should be either FINRA or the SEC. FINRA (http://www.finra.org) stands for the Financial Industry Regulatory Authority. SEC (https://www.sec.gov) stands for the Securities and Exchange Commission.

If the answer is FINRA, the advisor will hold some type of securities license and/or perhaps several licenses. To find out you can use the BrokerCheck (https://brokercheck.finra.org) feature on FINRA's website to see if there are any complaints on file.

If the answer is the SEC, you can use the feature on their website to check out both the advisor and the firm they work for.

Now you don't have to guess, or go with your gut, you can find out for sure if you are dealing with a straight shooter or someone who has had problems before. Their service is very affordable (about $50 to $100, cheap considering this could save you thousands) and can even be **free.** For example some "Financial Planners" have joined the National Ethics Bureau or the Advisor Check service voluntarily and willingly submitted to their vigorous background check. Why would any advisor submit to such a thorough background check and allow these companies to display this private information? Perhaps they have nothing to hide and by becoming a member they could offer some additional value to their clients. After all wouldn't you sleep better if you knew for sure that your financial advisor could be trusted and he/she had a flawless record of ethical business behavior? And the best part is that you can find these advisors for **free.** You don't have to pay for a background check you can just search and see if your advisor is already a member or you can look for a new advisor with a pre-checked flawless record who lives in your area. What a great service. Again you can't go by this alone as there are many advisors who have never gotten into any trouble but they still may be more of a product pusher or fee charger than a truly helpful professional but it can't hurt to know who you are dealing with before you trust them with your hard earned dollars. Another thing you will want to know about your advisor is how they get paid. Some advisors charge fees and some work mostly on commissions. Some people are under the false impression that just because someone charges a fee they are somehow magically more objective and ethical.

They reason that if the advisor works on fees then he will only recommend what is in their best interest as he has nothing to gain from recommending certain products. But remember everyone has a product to sell, even if that product is advice. In fact, many advisors that charge fees also collect commissions in addition to their fees. The important thing to keep in mind is that what makes someone honest and objective is their ethics not the way they get compensated for their work. So, make sure the person you are working with makes you feel comfortable and is not pressuring you to make decisions. All advisors will need to be paid one way or another.

If you are working with a fee based planner it is not uncommon to pay fees in excess of $5,000 or 1% or more each year of the money you invest whether he/she makes you money or loses it. One advantage of working with an advisor who works on commissions is that they are often willing to share their solutions with you without you having to make any financial commitments.

In other words, often the consultation and the planning are free because they will make money when you purchase the recommended products. For many products they get paid a finder's fee or a commission from the companies they represent. Would you rather pay them out of pocket or have them get paid by the companies they represent without taking money away from you? This is often a more practical solution for Middle American families living on a limited income who really can't afford a hefty planning fee.

Something else to look for is what type of advisor are they? Are they a generalist or a specialist? Ask the advisor what their typical client is like? If they do not know who they best serve then they are a generalist, like your general practitioner. Some advisors will focus on solving a particular problem or working with a particular group of people. If you fit into their niche you will more likely get better help with your goals. For example, if you go to an advisor to help you get out of debt so you can plan for retirement and they tell you they mainly work with people who are already retired and have a million dollar net worth then perhaps you are in the wrong office.

You may also want to ask your friends and family who they use. It is always a good idea to work from referral. Logic would have it that if they are doing a good job for your friend they should be capable of doing a good job for you. But even though I think this is a good idea, do not put too much weight on a recommendation. You need to check them out for yourself. Do a background check. Ask them what type of clients they work with most. Do they specialize, and so on? After all this is your financial future you are talking about.

To Sum Things Up

I truly hope you found this book to be valuable. Many of the points I have shared with you are a compellation of the many books I have read on these subjects coupled with my 16 years of experience of working with people just like you. I know what it is like to struggle financially. I know what it is like to dig yourself halfway out of a big pile of debt only to fall right back into it. I have spent many sleepless nights worrying about my finances and how I would be able to take care of my own family and provide for them. I have at times had to borrow from a credit card just to be able to pay my bills. I have also talked with and worked with hundreds of families who have these same struggles and worries and I have learned that there are better ways to manage your money where much of this stress can be relieved by just following some of the basic principles I have outlined in this book. This does not mean you will never again fall on hard times. My goal was to give you some tools so that the next time things get tough you will be in a much better position to weather the storm. Knowing that you are in that position or at least have a plan to get there will alleviate much of the worry that comes along with managing your finances. My hope is that once you have some of your basic needs met, like a solid emergency fund and the basic insurances to protect yourself and your family, you will worry a lot less about your money and learn to enjoy it.

Don't wait to use this information. If you're not sure how to apply it, read it over again or more importantly get some help. There are people out there in the financial services field who care and who are trained to give you the help and guidance you need. You don't need to be wealthy to have a financial plan. Remember that over your working life at least $1,000,000 or more will pass through your hands. How much of it will you keep? Now that you are armed with this vital financial information you have a choice. You can continue to follow the masses and end up like them. 96% of which will end up dependent on Social Security for income because they never did much planning. Or, you can chose to make every dollar you can manage work as hard for you as possible, as safely as possible, and with as little tax as possible. These goals are obtainable and you deserve to achieve them. I wish you all the best with all of your financial endeavors and I thank you for reading my book. If I can ever be of service please give me call.

About The Author...

Antonio Filippone, RFC, FMM
Registered Financial Consultant

Antonio "Tony" Filippone, specializes in consulting with middle American families helping them to get out of debt and save more for their financial goals without having to change their lifestyles to do it. Mr. Filippone has been interviewed on the ***Healthy, Wealthy and Wise*** Radio Show as well as locally on ***Live At Five*** with Dean Ervin and **Mortgage Talk** on **WROK News Talk Radio 1440AM.** He has also published numerous articles for highly acclaimed financial planning journals such as The ***Register***, ***The Financial Services Journal*** as well as many internet publications. In addition to being a published author and radio guest, Tony is also a well-known and respected speaker and has spoken as a financial expert at ***Rock Valley College*** as well as for the ***County of Winnebago*** while participating in ***Money Smart Week*** sponsored by the **Federal Reserve Bank of Chicago.**

Tony was raised on Long Island, NY where he grew up working in the Family Top Soil delivery business. It was real *"get your hands dirty work"* with heavy lifting and long hours but he learned what it meant to "work" for a living. It was this upbringing that inspired him to write a financial book that would appeal to other hard working, Middle American families.

Tony was the only member of his immediate family to graduate from college which he did in May of 1993. Almost immediately after graduation he was hired by a world-renowned financial services firm in New York where he successfully assisted many families to safely reach their financial goals. He has had a passion for helping Middle American families with their financial concerns ever since.

In 2001 Antonio and his wife Patricia decided they wanted to expand their family and so they moved to Rockford, IL where Patricia was originally from. They choose the Mid-West as the setting for them to raise their family due to the lower cost of living and the more relaxed pace of life. Antonio, Patricia and their two home schooled children Nino and Katie enjoy living in the Rockford area very much.

Are you happy with the amount of money you have been able to save? Contact Tony for more info on how you can improve your family's financial future.

Tony@RockfordRetirement.com
Phone (815) 633-9595

Made in the USA
Monee, IL
04 November 2026

67378038R00056